Number 104
Winter 2004

New Directions for Evaluation

Jean A. King
Editor-in-Chief

Robin Miller
Katherine Ryan
Nancy Zajano
Associate Editors

Ruth A. Bowan
Assistant Editor

International Perspectives on Evaluation Standards

Craig Russon
Gabrielle Russon
Editors

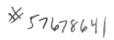

INTERNATIONAL PERSPECTIVES ON EVALUATION STANDARDS
Craig Russon, Gabrielle Russon (eds.)
New Directions for Evaluation, no. 104
Jean A. King, Editor-in-Chief
Copyright ©2005 Wiley Periodicals, Inc., A Wiley company

Microfilm copies of issues and articles are available in 16mm and 35mm, as well as microfiche in 105mm, through University Microfilms Inc., 300 North Zeeb Road, Ann Arbor, Michigan 48106-1346.

New Directions for Evaluation is indexed in Contents Pages in Education, Higher Education Abstracts, and Sociological Abstracts.

NEW DIRECTIONS FOR EVALUATION (ISSN 1097-6736, electronic ISSN 1534-875X) is part of The Jossey-Bass Education Series and is published quarterly by Wiley Subscription Services, Inc., a Wiley company, at Jossey-Bass, 989 Market Street, San Francisco, California 94103-1741.

SUBSCRIPTIONS cost $80.00 for U.S./Canada/Mexico; $104 international. For institutions, agencies, and libraries, $175 U.S.; $215 Canada; $249 international. Prices subject to change.

EDITORIAL CORRESPONDENCE should be addressed to the Editor-in-Chief, Jean A. King, University of Minnesota, 330 Wulling Hall, 86 Pleasant Street SE, Minneapolis, MN 55455.

www.josseybass.com

Editorial Policy and Procedures

New Directions for Evaluation, a quarterly sourcebook, is an official publication of the American Evaluation Association. The journal publishes empirical, methodological, and theoretical works on all aspects of evaluation. A reflective approach to evaluation is an essential strand to be woven through every volume. The editors encourage volumes that have one of three foci: (1) craft volumes that present approaches, methods, or techniques that can be applied in evaluation practice, such as the use of templates, case studies, or survey research; (2) professional issue volumes that present issues of import for the field of evaluation, such as utilization of evaluation or locus of evaluation capacity; (3) societal issue volumes that draw out the implications of intellectual, social, or cultural developments for the field of evaluation, such as the women's movement, communitarianism, or multiculturalism. A wide range of substantive domains is appropriate for *New Directions for Evaluation;* however, the domains must be of interest to a large audience within the field of evaluation. We encourage a diversity of perspectives and experiences within each volume, as well as creative bridges between evaluation and other sectors of our collective lives.

The editors do not consider or publish unsolicited single manuscripts. Each issue of the journal is devoted to a single topic, with contributions solicited, organized, reviewed, and edited by a guest editor. Issues may take any of several forms, such as a series of related chapters, a debate, or a long article followed by brief critical commentaries. In all cases, the proposals must follow a specific format, which can be obtained from the editor-in-chief. These proposals are sent to members of the editorial board and to relevant substantive experts for peer review. The process may result in acceptance, a recommendation to revise and resubmit, or rejection. However, the editors are committed to working constructively with potential guest editors to help them develop acceptable proposals.

Jean A. King, Editor-in-Chief
University of Minnesota
330 Wulling Hall
86 Pleasant Street SE
Minneapolis, MN 55455
e-mail: kingx004@umn.edu

CONTENTS

EDITORS' NOTES

The inaugural assembly of the International Organization for Cooperation in Evaluation (IOCE), a loose coalition of regional and national evaluation organizations from around the world, took place March 28–30, 2003, in Lima, Peru (Russon and Love, 2003). During the event, delegates from developing countries made several passionate pleas to improve the quality of evaluation. One told the story of an evaluation of a $10 million development program in Africa. She concluded, "The evaluation was done so badly that one could hardly understand the language in which it was written. The methodology was so flawed that in some cases, the managers of the program were not taken into account. The outcome of that evaluation was frighteningly bad. The program was closed down because the evaluator was an international person who did not understand the context whatsoever, [who] did not even have a clue."

Although this experience took place in an African country, it could easily have taken place anywhere in the world. Quality of evaluation is an issue that transcends regional and national boundaries. Evaluators have employed several strategies to address this concern: the formation of regional and national evaluation organizations, formal and informal training programs, and the accumulation of a body of professional literature (Stufflebeam, 1986). However, none of these strategies is likely to hold as much promise for improving the quality of evaluation as the development and application of standards.

Standards hold such promise because they establish a set of commonly agreed on principles for judging the quality of evaluation designs, practices, and reports. They provide guidance for developing evaluation training objectives and materials and for preparing evaluation contracts. They can help to explain evaluation and its uses to the public and to guide legal, administrative, and technical decisions about evaluations. In addition, standards can be helpful in interpreting and using evaluation reports; developing hypotheses and questions to guide research on evaluation; and extending the state of the art of evaluation through a working philosophy open to public scrutiny and debate (Stufflebeam, 1994).

Although the need for evaluation standards is universal, the approach to their development and application is not. With regard to development, some regional and national evaluation organizations have chosen to modify the U.S.-Canadian standards to fit their own cultural contexts. Others are developing standards purposefully independent of this preexisting counterpart. In

The views expressed in this volume represent those of the authors and not necessarily those of the W. K. Kellogg Foundation.

addition, some international agencies and funders have elected to develop their own sets of evaluation standards.

With regard to application, some evaluators favor setting up external mechanisms to police the system. Others, who reject such external intervention, think the solution is to promote the internalization of evaluation standards through professional development. There seems to be some agreement that consumer education would be beneficial. This would involve helping funders and governments apply standards to evaluation products that they receive from consultants to ensure that they are of high quality (Russon and Love, 2003).

Given the diversity of approaches to the development and application of standards, it is becoming increasingly clear that we have much to learn from each other. The purpose of this issue is to enable the international evaluation community, including U.S.-based members of the American Evaluation Association, to learn how evaluators in several countries are dealing with concerns associated with standards. This information may help readers to adapt techniques or ideas from countries other than their own or at least to be more aware of the choices they have implicitly made in their conceptualization and practice of evaluation.

The issue contains eight chapters that discuss efforts to create program evaluation standards (as opposed to personnel or student evaluation standards) undertaken by a broad cross-section of regional and national evaluation organizations, nongovernmental organizations, and governments. There are no chapters from Asia or Latin America because we were unaware of attempts to develop such standards in those regions. We believe that the cross-section represented in this issue fully demonstrates the diversity of approaches to this topic.

In Chapter One, Arnold Love and Craig Russon define what international evaluation standards mean—and also what they do not mean. They discuss the concept of open standards and identify and analyze major themes that emerged during the IOCE debates over standards.

In Chapter Two, Don Yarbrough, Lyn Shulha, and Flora Caruthers provide a historical perspective on the development of the Program Evaluation Standards. In addition, they discuss uses made of the standards during the past two decades, both in and outside the United States.

In Chapter Three, Thomas Widmer presents developments in selected Western European countries and the European Commission (EC) in the domain of evaluation standards since the beginning of the 1990s. The chapter explores similarities and differences in evaluation standard development among four European countries: Switzerland, Germany, France, and the United Kingdom.

Wolfgang Beywl and Sandra Speer in Chapter Four describe a Europe-wide empirical study on evaluation standards within the policy field of vocational education and training (VET). Following this, they reflect on evaluation standards used at different administrative levels of the EC.

The African Evaluation Guidelines are the topic of Chapter Five, by Jean-Charles Rouge. He begins by providing geographical and cultural information on Africa and then describes the evaluation context for the guidelines with special emphasis on the role of the African Evaluation Association. Following the description, he discusses the development of the guidelines, their implementation, and their use.

In Chapter Six, Doug Fraser uses the experience of the Australasian Evaluation Society to present an analysis of the important role that institutional factors can take, not only to the kinds of quality assurance that are considered desirable, but to whether collective standards emerge at all.

Jim Rugh discusses in Chapter Seven the process through which CARE staff developed the project Design, Monitoring, and Evaluation standards; the relevance of the content of the standards themselves; and the mainstreaming of their use throughout the seventy-two-nation CARE consortium.

In Chapter Eight, Craig Russon reports the results of an informal qualitative analysis of the chapters and provides summary reflection on the topic of international evaluation standards.

References

Russon, C., and Love, A. "The Inaugural Assembly of the International Organization for Cooperation in Evaluation: The Realization of a Utopian Dream." Kalamazoo: Evaluation Center, Western Michigan University, 2003.

Stufflebeam, D. L. "Standards of Practice for Evaluators." Paper presented at the annual meeting of the American Educational Research Association Symposium on Ethical Issues in Evaluative Research, San Francisco, 1986.

Stufflebeam, D. L. "Professional Standards for Educational Evaluation." In T. Husen, T. N. Postlethwaite, and H. J. Walberg (eds.), *International Encyclopedia of Education.* (2nd ed.) Oxford: Pergamon Press, 1994.

Craig Russon
Gabrielle Russon
Editors

CRAIG RUSSON is an evaluation manager with the W. K. Kellogg Foundation in Battle Creek, Michigan.

GABRIELLE RUSSON is a journalism student at Michigan State University. This issue marks her first editorial collaboration with her father.

1

This chapter discusses the general concept of international evaluation standards, describing the notion of open standards and the standards debate during two international meetings.

Evaluation Standards in an International Context

Arnold Love, Craig Russon

Over the past twenty years, the evaluation profession has struggled through several efforts to develop principles and standards, two closely related concepts. The dictionary definition of *principle* is "a comprehensive and fundamental law, doctrine, or assumption" (Merriam-Webster Online, 2004). In *The Program Evaluation Standards,* the Joint Committee on Standards for Educational Evaluation (1994) defines a *standard* as "a principle mutually agreed to by people engaged in the professional practice of evaluation, that, if met, will enhance the quality and fairness of an evaluation" (p. 2). Undergirding the concepts of both principles and standards is the concept of values. We believe that values are a particularly critical factor when considering evaluation standards within the international context.

For her chapter in *The Program Evaluation Standards in International Settings,* Taut (2000) conducted an extensive review of the cross-cultural psychological literature. She found that the concept of standards is inextricably linked to that of values and quoted Smith and Schwartz (1997): "As standards, cultural value priorities also influence how organizational performance is evaluated—for instance, in terms of productivity, social responsibility, innovativeness, or support for the existing power structure" (p. 83). Taut went on to point out that because standards are based on values and values differ from culture to culture, it is extremely difficult to transfer standards from one cultural context to another. Indeed, the Joint Committee has always maintained that its standards are distinctly North American and may not reflect the values, experiences, political realities, and practical constraints found in other countries. The committee has suggested explicitly that evaluation groups in other countries might choose to develop their own standards as a means of upgrading their evaluation practices (Stufflebeam, 1994).

Two Concepts Inappropriate to International Evaluation Contexts

In 1997, Chelimsky and Shadish wrote, "Evaluation is becoming increasingly international, but in ways that go beyond previous conceptions of what *international* means. *International* is no longer used only to describe the efforts of particular evaluators in individual countries around the world— although it certainly is still used this way. . . . Today, evaluation is also becoming international in the sense of being at the same time more indigenous, more global, and more transnational" (p. xi).

We agree with Chelimsky and Shadish that evaluation is becoming more international in the sense of being more indigenous. We can identify many evaluation concepts that originated outside North America (for example, participatory evaluation) that have received broad dissemination, thus enriching evaluation practice around the world (Conner and Hendricks, 1989). However, we also believe that applying the concepts of globalization and transnationalism to evaluation in general and to the development and use of standards in particular is inappropriate.

The concept of globalization is very muddy, and everyone defines it to his or her convenience (G. Raj, personal communication to C. Russon, Sept. 2004). However, globalization is often associated with the imposition of austere economic policies by international funding bodies on developing countries. Some view this as lacking in democracy, transparency, and social justice—values that are fundamental to the concept of evaluation (Korten, 1995). Also, some see standardization and uniformity as an almost inevitable outcome of globalization (Korten, 1995). This point is well illustrated by the initial reticence of African Evaluation Association organizers to participate in international initiatives because of concern over a loss of diversity: "There is a fear that Western evaluation theory and practice may supplant indigenous theory and practice of evaluation" (Love and Russon, 2000, p. 452).

A similar problem emerges with the concept of transnationalism. In macroeconomics, transnationalism is a label commonly applied to organizations that operate in multiple countries but have no allegiance to any of them (Korten, 1995). Transnational organizations may choose to claim local citizenship when that posture suits their purposes. However, any local commitments are typically temporary. Transnational organizations actively attempt to eliminate considerations of nationality in their efforts to maximize the opportunities that centralized global operations make possible. By eliminating national considerations, they are often able to avoid accountability for the harmful effects of their operations on society and the environment

(Korten, 1995). In other words, although evaluation standards are one way to promote accountability for the public welfare, transnationalism is often employed as a corporate strategy to do exactly the opposite, that is, to evade accountability. Thus, in international evaluation contexts, the conceptual application of either globalization or transnationalism to evaluation in general or to standards development in particular would be problematic.

Universal Standards versus Open Standards

If the concepts of globalization and transnationalism were to be applied to evaluation, it would probably be through the creation of universal evaluation standards. To understand how this could work, it is instructive to look at how "universal" standards have been implemented in trade and commerce by the World Trade Organization (WTO). Two main international bodies on which the WTO relies to set standards are the Codex Alimentarius Commission and the International Organization for Standardization (ISO). Both bodies are heavily influenced by the industries to which their standards apply and operate mainly behind closed doors (Constantini, 2001).

The WTO constrains its members from adopting standards stronger— from the point of view of the environment or public health and safety—than those set by the Codex Alimentarius or ISO. This imposition of ceilings, rather than floors, puts downward pressure on countries to harmonize (that is, to become uniform) national standards in areas covered by international standards. Such requirements tend to reduce national standards to the least common denominator (Constantini, 2001).

Application of the WTO model could mean the development of universal evaluation standards with few opportunities for important stakeholders to provide input. This set of universal evaluation standards would supersede the standards of all regional and national evaluation organizations. Effectively it would transfer decision-making power about standards from regional and national evaluation organizations to a body that is not directly accountable to members of those organizations. Finally, universal evaluation standards could put a ceiling on the ability of regional and national evaluation organizations to promote high-quality evaluation through the application and use of standards.

Juxtaposed to universal evaluation standards is the concept of open standards. The term *open standards* refers to two key attributes, openness in the standard-setting process, and open access to the standards themselves, so that evaluators and clients alike can use or modify them freely. The heart of the open standards process is a broad-based collaborative effort by diverse parties to develop consensus on terminology and the specifications for critical applications of the standards. Adopting an open standards process for international evaluation standards holds the potential to improve the quality of evaluation in a wide variety of settings, furthering the common objectives of evaluation networks and organizations worldwide.

Though not by original intent or design, the world is already using a de facto system of open evaluation standards. The Program Evaluation Standards (see Chapter Two) have been translated into many languages. In addition, several countries and regions have used the North American standards as the point of departure for their own efforts to develop standards appropriate for their cultural contexts. Several of these efforts are described in subsequent chapters of this issue.

Chapters Five and Seven, which deal, respectively, with Africa and CARE International, discuss standards that transcend national boundaries. The African Evaluation Association and CARE International, however, are not examples of transnational organizations. Rather, they are examples of multinational organizations. Like their counterpart, multinational organizations operate in multiple countries. But rather than attempting to eliminate considerations of nationality, multinational organizations take on a national identity in each country in which they operate and often try to present themselves as good corporate citizens in each locality.

Open standards eliminate the necessity of reinventing the wheel as users identify and modify existing standards to fit different values, cultural realities, and approaches to evaluation. This creates the opportunity for evaluators to strengthen the quality of their evaluations and their ability to meet the diverse needs of the end users by adapting the open standards as they see fit. For complex evaluations involving multiple sites, multiple jurisdictions, or multiple countries, open standards provide a way of fostering coordination and communication among evaluation teams, thereby making better use of indigenous evaluation capability and scarce evaluation resources.

International Organization for Cooperation in Evaluation

As more and more countries have undertaken standards development, standards have come into the purview of the recently launched International Organization for Cooperation in Evaluation (IOCE), a loose coalition of some fifty regional and national evaluation organizations from around the world (www.ioce.org). Program evaluation standards were a topic of debate during both the strategic planning meeting that took place in Barbados, West Indies, and the inaugural assembly of the IOCE.

In February 1999, a planning group held a residency meeting in Barbados to discuss issues associated with the formation of the coalition (Mertens and Russon, 2000). The leaders of fifteen regional and national evaluation organizations from around the world attended the meeting. Also in attendance were observers from the W. K. Kellogg Foundation, the University of the West Indies, the Caribbean Development Bank, and the U.N. Capital Development Fund.

During the meeting, one of the issues around which lively debate ensued was application of the Program Evaluation Standards to regions outside North America. On behalf of their respective evaluation organizations, several of the leaders from developing countries expressed a desire to undertake projects to create similar standards suitable for use in their own cultural contexts as a means to guide practice in their countries. Some leaders from evaluation organizations in developed countries, however, expressed their skepticism about evaluation standards in general. Some of them viewed standards as a barrier to innovation. In their view, the word *standards* implied an imposition of best practices, that is, a perceived "one best" approach. Furthermore, they thought that no one model could apply to all evaluations. As a result of the debate, the participants at the Barbados meeting delegated resolution of the issue by saying that it was not appropriate to make a determination regarding this matter at the international level. Rather, each country should make its own decision.

At the IOCE inaugural assembly, which took place four years later in Lima, Peru, the topic of standards was once again a topic of extensive debate (Russon and Love, 2003). The inaugural assembly was attended by forty leaders from twenty-six regional and national evaluation organizations from around the world, and as the opening story in the Editors' Notes documents, some of the participants from developing countries told disquieting stories about the ways that they had seen evaluation abused. The assembly recognized the need for mechanisms to improve the quality of international evaluations. One way proposed to accomplish this was through the development and use of evaluation standards.

Discussion of the issue dealt with two approaches that might be undertaken. Some delegates favored establishing external mechanisms to police the system. According to proponents, the system might take the form of "creating some kind of environment in which people would be aware that there are principles and learning and an environment that shapes expectations and there are mechanisms by which these expectations are communicated" (C. Russon, personal notes taken during the IOCE inaugural assembly).

Those who rejected external intervention thought the solution was to promote the internalization of local evaluation standards through professional development. These representatives saw internalization of standards as going hand-in-hand with efforts to promote the ethical practice of evaluation. The group seemed to agree that consumer education would be beneficial (Russon and Love, 2003). This would involve helping funders and governments apply standards to evaluation products that they receive from consultants to ensure that they are of high quality.

Major Themes from the IOCE Debates

An analysis of the IOCE debates points to four themes: the benefits and costs of standards, professional development, the relation of standards to ethical statements, and the presumed value of consumer education.

Figure 1.1. Continua of Costs and Benefits of Evaluation Standards

Benefits	Costs
Society	
Protection of society from harmful effects	Stifling of creative development
Profession	
Normative frameworks	Limits to individual freedoms
Individuals	
Improved social program benefits	Opportunity costs

Benefits and Costs of Standards. During the Barbados meeting, evaluation leaders identified the potential benefits of evaluation standards (for example, guide to practice, improvement of quality) that must be weighed against any potential costs (for example, barrier to innovation, imposition of perceived best practices, unequal application to all evaluations). These benefits and costs appear to fall along continua in a hierarchy of levels (Stake, 1981) of society, the profession, and individuals (see Figure 1.1). In this section, the benefits will be weighed against the costs at each level, followed by a brief discussion of the primacy of the hierarchy's levels.

At the societal level, there is a continuum with the protection of society from harmful effects of bad evaluation at one end. Harmful effects might include such things as eliminating the funding of a program that serves society's broader interests. At the other end of the continuum is the prospect of stifling the development of creative evaluation approaches and methods that might ultimately benefit society. Logic suggests that it is necessary to find a balance between the two ends of the continuum. It is clearly important to protect society from bad evaluation, but not at the expense of research and development on effective evaluation.

At the professional level, there is a continuum with normative frameworks at one end of the spectrum. Normative frameworks are important because they can guide practice, a benefit that most evaluation leaders in Barbados deemed important. They are also a mechanism for socializing novice evaluators. At the other end of the continuum are limits to individual freedoms. Our normative frameworks must not be so coercive that they threaten the nonconforming but effective evaluator. Logic would suggest that once again, it is necessary to find a balance between the two ends of the continuum. We need to find ways to help people socialize new evaluators to good practice while not stopping experienced evaluators from great practice.

At the individual level, there is a continuum with improved social program benefits at one end. The ultimate test of evaluation standards is whether they contribute to better-quality outcomes and delivery of services to individual stakeholders. If this does not happen, then the public and evaluators alike may see evaluation standards as leading to the misdirection of public funds, away from effective programming to ineffective bureaucratic processes. In contrast to the other levels, there is no balance to be sought on this continuum. Evaluation standards must help maximize benefits from improved social programs and minimize any opportunity costs that may be involved.

The view that one takes of the primacy of the levels in the hierarchy is undoubtedly influenced by the values one holds. Hofstede (1980) provides a framework for analyzing such value positions. Those who view the potential benefits to society and, to a certain extent, the profession as being the most important factor in decisions made about evaluation standards probably have a collectivist value position (Hofstede, 1980). Conversely, those who view the potential benefits to the individual as being the most important factor in the decisions made about evaluation standards probably hold an individualist value position (Hofstede, 1980). For example, in his critique of the Joint Committee's initial effort to develop the North American evaluation standards over twenty-five years ago, Stake (1981) wrote, "By my reasoning, it is the well-being of individual 'stakeholders' in society, not the well-being of the society nor the well being of the profession that justifies the organized imposition of constraints on individual evaluators" (p. 150). Stake thus makes it clear that he views the primacy of the individual level over the societal and professional levels, an individualist value position. To be certain, neither value position—collectivist or individualist—is correct or incorrect; this, rather, is a dimension that contributes to the shape and diversity of evaluation standards.

The Role of Professional Development. Delegates put forward two general approaches for applying standards during the debates at the IOCE inaugural assembly. The first was to police the system, which we generally view as an exercise in coercion and, in any case, expensive and unfeasible. The second approach was to promote the internalization of local evaluation standards through professional development. Stake (1981) wrote that the best standards are those that are internal within individuals and implicit in their work. However, because standards do not arise spontaneously within individual evaluators but require some external inputs, the promotion of professional development seems a sensible route for the near future.

In general, international professional development opportunities fall along a time continuum of short, medium, and long term. Short-term professional development would include the informal, nondegree, professional development sessions offered prior to conferences that regional and national evaluation organizations sponsor. For example, the Niger Monitoring and Evaluation Network (ReNSE) held a one-day training session in August 2004 that aimed at strengthening the capacities of ReNSE working group coordinators in the field of program evaluation standards, especially on the implementation and use of the African Evaluation Guidelines (AEG). The agenda included a presentation on AEG followed by application to several case studies and debate among the participants (J. C. Rouge, message to the XCeval listserv, Aug. 2004).

An example of medium-term professional development would be the World Bank's International Program for Development Evaluation Training (IPDET). This joint collaboration between the World Bank Operations Evaluation and Carleton University is designed to meet the professional development needs of governments, as well as the needs of professional evaluators working in bilateral and multilateral development agencies and banks. A review of the 2004 IPDET program schedule showed that evaluation standards, particularly those of the Development Assistance Committee of the Organization for Economic Cooperation and Development, are among the first topics in the four-week program of study (World Bank, 2004). Another example of medium-term professional development that integrates standards and ethical guidelines into its basic courses in program evaluation is the Essential Skills Series of the Canadian Evaluation Society.

An example of long-term professional development would be any formal degree program in program evaluation or evaluation studies. One innovative example would be the multidisciplinary Ph.D. program offered through The Evaluation Center at Western Michigan University. As part of the program, each student is required to demonstrate knowledge of general evaluation theory, methodology, and practice issues, as well as the ability to apply evaluation to his or her chosen area of specialization. The minimum required competencies include the use of professional evaluation standards and checklists for evaluation and metaevaluation (Evaluation Center, 2004).

Ethical Statements as Functional Standards Documents. The evaluation leaders who attended the Barbados meeting and the IOCE inaugural assembly saw standards as going hand-in-hand with efforts to promote the ethical practice of evaluation. One manner in which regional and national evaluation organizations have accomplished this is by putting forward ethical statements. (According to the definition of evaluation standards already provided in this chapter, these ethical statements can well be considered standards. However, due to space constraints, we decided to focus on a subset of standards and excluded ethical statements.) The American Evaluation Association's "Guiding Principles" were an early attempt to promote ethical behavior. The document contains five principles: (1) Systematic Inquiry, (2) Competence, (3) Integrity/Honesty, (4) Respect for People, and (5) Responsibilities for the General and Public Welfare. The Canadian Evaluation Association adopted its "Guidelines for Ethical Conduct" in 1996. The document contains three guidelines: (1) Competence, (2) Integrity, and (3) Accountability.

The Australasian Evaluation Society has made an extensive effort to promote ethics. In 1997, it endorsed its "Guidelines for the Ethical Conduct of Evaluations." The preface of the document is devoted to the background, purpose, scope, audience, relationship to other guidelines, approach, and terminology. The document contains three principles that deal with critical phases of the evaluation process: (1) Commissioning and Preparing for an Evaluation, (2) Conducting an Evaluation, and (3) Reporting the Results of an Evaluation. Each principle has several guidelines associated with it.

Guidelines deal with such matters as contract negotiations, changes to the contract, potential risks, competence, conflict of interest, and conducting one's self in an honorable manner. Altogether there are twenty-two guidelines.

Even newly formed regional and national evaluation organizations have addressed the issue of ethics. The International Program Evaluation Network (Georgia, Moldova, Russia, and Ukraine) has adopted a set of five Program Evaluation Principles: (1) program evaluation can be based only on accurate and reliable information; (2) evaluation should be competent; (3) program evaluators guarantee honesty and transparency throughout evaluation; (4) program evaluators respect safety and dignity of people with whom they cooperate in the course of their professional activity; and (5) evaluators have professional obligations determined by public interests and public welfare.

The Importance of Consumer Education. No regional or national evaluation organization currently has a credentialing, certification, or licensure program in place. This means that there are no formal mechanisms to ensure that consumers have engaged a qualified evaluator. Therefore, the old dictum "buyer beware" continues to apply to evaluation. For this reason, the evaluation leaders at both the Barbados meeting and the IOCE inaugural assembly saw consumer education as potentially beneficial.

The ultimate goal of such education would be for consumers to be facile enough with a set of standards appropriate for their cultural context that they could conduct a metaevaluation. The term *metaevaluation* refers to the evaluation of an evaluation (Joint Committee on Standards for Educational Evaluation, 1994). There are two general types of metaevaluation: formative and summative (Joint Committee on Standards for Educational Evaluation, 1994). Formative metaevaluation guides the planning and implementation of a program evaluation. Summative metaevaluation assesses the worth and merit of a completed program evaluation.

Speaking from our own experience with international development agencies, we believe that formative metaevaluation is a much more effective focus. It offers a greater likelihood that the program evaluation will ultimately be successful. For example, international development agencies that wait to conduct summative metaevaluation often find themselves in a dilemma. There are regularly instances in which the final report is of poor quality, yet all the funds from the contract have been expended. The agencies are left with two difficult choices: provide supplemental funds to fix the report, which is sometimes difficult for a contractor to do without going back and redoing the entire evaluation, or not pay the contractor, something that is also difficult to do if all of the terms of reference have otherwise been met.

A Final Word

This chapter has provided definitions of terms and identified major themes and points of debate that arise in the subsequent chapters. We believe that readers will see these themes and points of debate come up time and time again within the frame of the common set of issues addressed by the authors. Chapter Eight reports the results of a qualitative analysis of the chapters.

References

Chelimsky, E., and Shadish, W. "Preface." In E. Chelimsky and W. Shadish (eds.), *Evaluation for the Twenty-First Century.* Thousand Oaks, Calif.: Sage, 1997.

Conner, R., and Hendricks, M. (eds.). *International Innovations in Evaluation Methodology.* New Directions for Program Evaluation, no. 42. San Francisco: Jossey-Bass, 1989.

Constantini, P. "You Must Lower National Standards If They Are Higher Than International Standards: What's Wrong with the WTO." 2001. [www.speakeasy.org/-peterc/wtow/wto-stds.htm].

Evaluation Center. "Program Requirements." 2004. [http://evaluation.wmich.edu/phd/requirements/index.htm].

Hofstede, G. *Culture's Consequences: International Differences in Work-Related Values.* Thousand Oaks, Calif.: Sage, 1980.

Joint Committee on Standards for Educational Evaluation. *The Program Evaluation Standards: How to Assess Evaluations of Educational Programs.* (2nd ed.) Thousand Oaks, Calif.: Sage, 1994.

Korten, D. C. *When Corporations Rule the World.* West Hartford, Conn.: Kumarian Press and Berrett-Koehler, 1995.

Love, A., and Russon, C. "Building a Worldwide Evaluation Community: Past, Present, and Future." *Evaluation and Program Planning: An International Journal,* 2000, *23,* 449–459.

Merriam-Webster Online. "Principle." 2004. [www.m-w.com/cgi-bin/dictionary?book=Dictionary&va=principle].

Mertens, D., and Russon, C. "A Proposal for the International Organization for Cooperation in Evaluation." *American Journal of Evaluation,* 2000, *21,* 275–284.

Russon, C., and Love, A. "The Inaugural Assembly of the International Organization for Cooperation in Evaluation: The Realization of a Utopian Dream." Kalamazoo: Evaluation Center, Western Michigan University, 2003.

Smith, P. B., and Schwartz, S. H. "Values." In J. W. Berry, M. H. Segall, and C. Kagitcibasi (eds.), *Handbook of Cross-Cultural Psychology.* (2nd ed.) Needham Heights, Mass.: Allyn & Bacon, 1997.

Stake, R. E. "Setting Standards for Educational Evaluators." *Evaluation News,* 1981, *2,* 149–152.

Stufflebeam, D. L. "Professional Standards for Educational Evaluation." In T. Husen, T. N. Postlethwaite, and H. J. Walberg (eds.), *International Encyclopedia of Education.* (2nd ed.) Oxford, England: Pergamon Press, 1994.

Taut, S. "Cross-Cultural Transferability of the Program Evaluation Standards." In C. Russon (ed.), *The Program Evaluation Standards in International Settings.* Kalamazoo: Evaluation Center, Western Michigan University, 2000.

World Bank, Operations Evaluation Department. *International Program for Development Evaluation Training 2004.* Washington, D.C.: World Bank, 2004.

ARNOLD LOVE *is an independent program evaluation consultant based in Toronto, Canada.*

CRAIG RUSSON *is an evaluation manager with the W. K. Kellogg Foundation in Battle Creek, Michigan.*

2

To ground the discussion of standards in an international context, this chapter traces the continuing history of the U.S.-Canadian Joint Committee Standards.

Background and History of the Joint Committee's Program Evaluation Standards

Donald B. Yarbrough, Lyn M. Shulha, Flora Caruthers

It is generally thought that evaluation originated with the civil service exams that were administered in ancient China. However, modern evaluation and, of particular importance to this chapter, evaluation standards originated in the United States. Why this occurred is part of a larger question about the development of social and educational programs in the United States and the demand for effective and efficient evaluation of them.

Origins of the *Program Evaluation Standards* in the United States

A number of thorough introductions to the origins of program evaluation in the United States have been published (Rossi, Lipsey, and Freeman, 2004; Fitzpatrick, Sanders, and Worthen, 2004; King, 2003). These highlight the development in the first half of the twentieth century of methods to describe and assess educational and social program outcomes through the precise specification and measurement of objectives (Tyler, 1942). They also describe the rise of federal, state, and local interest in funding educational programs and social programs in the second half of the twentieth century (Rossi, Lipsey, and Freeman, 2004; Fitzpatrick, Sanders, and Worthen, 2004; Shadish, Cook, and Leviton, 1991; Stufflebeam, 2003, 2004). Several factors—the large number of new social and educational programs in the United States, the development of measurement and assessment technology, the belief in human and societal improvement, and the demands for accountability regarding public expenditures—set the stage for the development of standards to guide program evaluations.

The development of standards for evaluating programs and projects grew out of situations and circumstances that were characteristic of, if not unique to, the American experience. (In this chapter, we use *American* to refer explicitly to citizens of the United States. An alternative might be *North American*, which would also include citizens of Canada and Mexico.) American identity has historically included a belief that American citizens, regardless of their circumstances, can reach their economic, societal, and personal goals through their own abilities and hard work.

Many Americans firmly believe in the possibility of personal and societal improvement. Indeed, some Americans consider achieving these goals to be a personal duty. Furthermore, America has been and still is in some fundamental sense a meritocracy. As early as the nineteenth century, it was apparent to many Europeans that a defining characteristic of the United States was its emphasis on individuals' abilities and the value of individual merit. Many Americans believed that they could rise above humble origins through ingenuity in using and exploiting vast lands and resources to achieve wealth, power, and status (de Tocqueville, 2004). Even at the start of the twenty-first century with many aspects of American expansionism in question, most Americans still expect to be able to achieve in accordance with their abilities and efforts rather than their backgrounds of origin. At the same time, many Americans recognize the need for compensatory programs because not all citizens have access to the same opportunities to learn and develop and not all experience the same status and privilege (Mark, Henry, and Julnes, 2000).

This need for fair opportunities to learn and develop in a meritocracy provides a powerful incubator for programs to improve society and individual development. The large number of such programs also creates the need for effective and efficient evaluations to help improve those many programs and to document their worth to society (Fitzpatrick, Sanders, and Worthen, 2004; Rossi, Lipsey, and Freeman, 2004).

Rise of Standardized Testing. In the early and mid-twentieth century, with the dissemination of technology to measure human characteristics and aptitudes through standardized tests and "scientific" observations, social scientists and educators gained new tools. This technology gained widespread use for describing individual ability and program outcomes. The belief was that more precise, scientific measurement could lead to societal improvement through improved description, planning, and outcomes assessment. Standardized testing technology promised objective descriptions of existing abilities and achievements at regular intervals, allowing inferences about individuals' merit and worth along specific dimensions so that decision makers could rationally select individuals for specific jobs or for participation in tailored programs. In addition, because testers could administer measures in time series, this technology promised a relatively dependable mechanism to draw conclusions about systematic efforts to improve children's academic skills or the outcomes of other tailored social or educational programs. In the context of the American educational system, the need to compare individuals with one another and programs with one another for accountability purposes found a rational basis in testing technology.

Increases in Social and Educational Programming. We cannot know whether the growth of testing technology in America fueled a growth in social and educational programming and a stronger belief in social and individual improvement, or whether the existing strong belief in the improvability of human conditions led inexorably to a technology to help document the outcomes of efforts to do so. In either case, the periods after the Great Depression and World War II in the United States led to unprecedented levels of programming to improve all aspects of American life, as well as to rebuild Europe and other regions that had been economically, politically, and socially devastated. On the international front, the Marshall Plan invested significant resources to build nations and spread capitalistic democracy. In the United States, social programming efforts continued and produced such notable innovations as universal social security and the GI bill.

With the advent of the Great Society programs and the War on Poverty in the mid-1960s, the proliferation of educational and social programming at the state and local levels dramatically increased the need for large numbers of program evaluations (Worthen, Sanders, and Fitzpatrick, 1997). That demand was fueled in large part by budget lines mandating evaluations of funded programs. At the same time, there was no well-developed evaluation profession. Social science researchers and educators from various disciplines soon became engaged in the practice of program and project evaluation, borrowing directly what they had learned from conducting their paradigmatic research or from their knowledge of educational and psychological testing. Initially, they were unable to adequately adapt and modify their methodologies and approaches (Rossi, Lipsey, and Freeman, 2004; Fitzpatrick, Sanders, and Worthen, 2004; Stufflebeam, 2004). Out of this crucible came many faulty program evaluations and increased scholarship on program and project evaluation methodology (Weiss, 1972; Scriven, 1967; Stufflebeam, 1967). Numerous evaluators noticed the difficulty of implementing research designs in field settings (Cronbach, 1982; Rossi, Lipsey, and Freeman, 2004) and the limited use of evaluation results in decision making (Weiss, 1998; Patton, 1997).

Development of Program Evaluation and the Program Evaluation Standards. American researchers and educators were inventing the program evaluation profession on the basis of existing social science research methodologies. For American social scientists, this challenge was unprecedented. The originators of American branches of many social science research areas in education, psychology, philosophy, and sociology had always relied heavily on the research and theories of accessible thinkers from other nations, especially the European-Western traditions (Hergenhahn, 2001). However, the sheer volume of programming made possible by the unique role of the United States after World War II had no parallel. American researchers who took on the task of program and project evaluation could not look to an established practice field elsewhere in the world. In a real sense, the practice of program evaluation and the necessary theory and research to inform it, set as it was in the unique political context of the times, had to be developed in the United States.

In contrast to program evaluation as a practice field, the theories and methodologies of psychometrics and testing technology had their well-developed roots in European psychophysics and had achieved disciplinary status in American academia. Although methodology for test use in evaluating person characteristics was well established scientifically, in theory and in practice, the notion of using tests to help improve programs or to hold them accountable was not so clear-cut. For example, complexity in modeling the reliability of group scores traditionally has received scant attention even though seminal research on the reliability of tests for individual differences found widespread audiences in the first half of the twentieth century (Feldt and Brennan, 1993; Cronbach, 1951; Brennan, 2001).

In the early 1970s, when representatives from the American Educational Research Association, the American Psychological Association, and the National Council on Measurement in Education met to revise and update a set of standards for testing and test use, they visited the topic of program evaluation but recommended that a separate subcommittee be created to deal with program evaluation and personnel evaluation. Under the leadership of Daniel L. Stufflebeam, an active program evaluation practitioner and theoretician, this subcommittee developed into the Joint Committee on Standards for Educational Evaluation (JCSEE) in 1975 (Joint Committee on Standards for Educational Evaluation, 1981, 1994; Stufflebeam, 2003). The subcommittee concluded that wider representation was needed to capture the diverse perspectives and contributions of program evaluation stakeholders across the United States. By the time the JCSEE completed and published the *Standards for Evaluations of Educational Programs, Projects, and Materials,* the JCSEE included members from twelve national professional organizations (JCSEE, 1981).

The first edition of the *Program Evaluation Standards* incorporated the practice and theoretical knowledge about program evaluation available at the time (Stufflebeam, 2003; Thompson, 1994). Standards were organized into four major areas of concern experienced by the first generations of program evaluators: how to make evaluations more useful and more often used (utility), how to conduct program evaluations feasibly in the real world where little can be completely controlled and politically difficult situations abound (feasibility), how to ensure propriety in all aspects of the evaluation (propriety), and how to promote accurate and dependable evaluations (accuracy). These were described as "four main concerns about any evaluation" (JCSEE, 1981, p. 1). The *Program Evaluation Standards* made clear that not all standards were equally applicable in all situations and that professional judgment should be brought to bear on all aspects of program evaluation, including whether and how to apply specific standards in specific evaluation situations.

Even as the field of evaluation has expanded, this general organization into four clusters of issues and concerns has remained. The second edition of the *Program Evaluation Standards* (JCSEE, 1994) maintained this overarching organization, as did the other two JCSEE volumes: *Personnel Evaluation Standards* (JCSEE, 1988) and *Student Evaluation Standards* (JCSEE, 2003). At JCSEE meetings, however, the continued use of this organization has been a topic for discussion. To date, it remains a useful organizing framework for evaluation standards in the continued judgment of the JCSEE. However, with each new set of standards or subsequent revision, the JCSEE solicits comments and opinions of all stakeholders and users of the different standards and revisits the issue of this organization.

Conditions for and Changes in the *Program Evaluation Standards,* Second Edition

In the fifteen-year span between the drafts of the first and second editions, many circumstances and conditions changed. There was dramatic growth in the practice of evaluation in the United States and in the teaching and mentoring of graduate students and professionals who wanted to become program evaluation practitioners. Many more students from abroad came to the United States to study educational measurement, psychometrics, and other social sciences, and many completed their first courses in program evaluation and had their first introductions to its practice in U.S. locales. More and more evaluators trained in the United States took on the role of consultants abroad or conducted evaluations in international settings. In 1986, the two separate U.S. evaluation professional groups, the Evaluation Network and the Evaluation Research Society, merged to become the American Evaluation Association (AEA), which assumed responsibility for the publication of the existing journals, *Evaluation News* (renamed *Evaluation Practice*) and *New Directions for Program Evaluation* (later renamed *New Directions for Evaluation*). In the early 1990s, the AEA and the Canadian Evaluation Society began planning for the first international conference on evaluation, which took place in Vancouver, British Columbia, in 1995.

In that fifteen-year span, the literature on the theory and practice of program evaluation increased dramatically. Suitable textbooks for introductory courses gained wider circulation (Rossi, 1982; Worthen and Sanders, 1987) and programs for the study of evaluation, in conjunction with other academic specialties, made their way into the graduate school curriculum. Books and articles appeared that fundamentally questioned the scientific bases of evaluation and the assumptions underlying psychometrics and educational testing (Guba and Lincoln, 1989).

At the time of the writing of the first edition of the *Program Evaluation Standards,* the JCSEE included or had direct access to most of the leading practitioners and thinkers in the nascent field of program evaluation. By the time of the second edition, the annual meetings of AEA had grown from a few hundred to more than a thousand. The organization evolved to include a number of topical interest groups (TIGs) to provide a collaborative setting for particular professional and practical interest areas. The TIG on qualitative methods increased in size until it was larger than the quantitative methods TIG. Voices addressing the needs of underrepresented positions and diverse populations had become prominent, and, in general, the field of evaluation practice and theory was rapidly expanding. This dramatic growth created a situation where the JCSEE, even after increasing membership to fourteen U.S. and two Canadian national professional organizations at the time of the second edition, needed a process that ensured an opportunity for all interested parties to contribute suggestions to a second edition of the *Program Evaluation Standards.*

A major change prior to the second edition was American National Standards Institute (ANSI) accreditation in 1988 of JCSEE procedures (Sanders, 1994), which led to the certification of the second edition of *Program Evaluation Standards* as definitive American National Standards. Many of the ANSI-accredited procedures were similar to the procedures followed for the first edition (JCSEE, 1981) and are well documented in publications of the time (Sanders, 1994). The ten components of the ANSI process (Sanders, 1994) emphasized the need for widespread review, including international review, and for multiple national hearings to gather as extensive a body of suggestions and comments as possible. The process was described as "public, participatory, open, and consensual," in keeping with ANSI principles (Sanders, 1994, p. 1). JCSEE work and documents stated that the Program Evaluation Standards were considered a living set of standards to be used, evaluated, clarified, and updated regularly in response to the needs and feedback from users. In addition, the Program Evaluation Standards in both editions described explicit mechanisms for ongoing coordination and mutual exchange with other organizations and their standards and guiding principles (JCSEE, 1981, 1994).

Although many of the procedures and the general organization into four areas of concern were consistent from the first to the second edition, there were notable changes (JCSEE, 1994). The standards as first developed (JCSEE, 1981) were distinctly focused on educational evaluations in schools. After publication of the first edition, evaluators in other domains expressed interest in using the standards. The second edition broadened its focus to include applications in such areas as higher education, medicine and health care, business, social service agencies, and the military. In addition, it reflected both theoretical and practical developments in American evaluation in the decade after the first edition's publication. In contrast to the first edition, which referenced no supporting documentation, the second edition provided explicit citations for each standard. More extensive cases were added, and many aspects of the original were updated and made more nuanced to reflect changes in theory and practice. It included the "Functional Table of Contents" to facilitate differing uses and modified explications for each standard. Other changes reflected attempts to increase the utility of the standards through improved organization and content.

Revising the *Program Evaluation Standards*, Second Edition

The second edition of *Program Evaluation Standards* is ten years old, and preparations have begun for the third edition. Over the past decade, the JCSEE has invited all users of the *Program Evaluation Standards* to contribute suggestions for improving the standards. That invitation has now moved into a more active phase. Currently, a JCSEE task force that we comprise is conducting an assessment of the need for specific revisions to any and all aspects of the *Program Evaluation Standards*. We are relying on surveys of members of all sponsoring organizations as well as other interested evaluation stakeholders; available documents, including published program evaluations and scholarship on the practice of evaluation and theoretical and research foundations; formal and informal interviews; other committee and subcommittee recommendations; and any published or otherwise available critiques of the standards or recommendations for maintenance and improvement of the standards from practicing evaluators, theorists, and program evaluation stakeholders. The individual elements in this corpus of informative materials will be referenced in the next revision and to the extent possible archived with the JCSEE.

In evaluating the second edition, we are asking for the most pressing needs that the current standards and ancillary materials are and are not meeting. The primary intended users for the proposed ANSI-approved third edition of *Program Evaluation Standards* will be those with a stake in North American programs and program evaluation activities and those who are part of the ANSI review process, including international reviewers. However, now more than ever before in our global villages and globalized world, American evaluators are aspiring to practice in ways that recognize diversity in the evaluation setting. This need is significant for, but not limited to, those whose work extends into multicultural, multinational, and international contexts (Thompson-Robinson, Hopson, and SenGupta, 2004; Russon, 2000). It is not unusual for educational and social programs, both domestic and foreign, to be conceptualized and evaluated by those whose experiences differ significantly from those of intended program personnel and users. While the dangers in this gap are regularly identified, there is no doubt that, on its completion, users of the third edition of *Program Evaluation Standards* will be practicing at a time when the skills and sensitivities required to assess the richness, complexity, and consequences of such programs will be at a premium. With regard to instrumental, conceptual, or process uses (Weiss, 1998; Thompson, 1994; Patton, 1997), then the practices of North American evaluators and the consequences of North American evaluation practices and practice guidelines often reach far beyond North America, not only in direct impact on programs on the practice of evaluation but also through effects on how other cultural and national groups think about evaluation and its potential for increasing social good (Mark, Henry, and Julnes, 2000).

ANSI procedures mandate an international review because ANSI standards guide the development of products that have international as well as national use. In today's world, an international perspective would be highly desirable even if the standards development process were limited to U.S. constituents. In the past, the perspectives guiding program evaluation may have comfortably been limited primarily to those of established majority groups. Today, we need a better understanding of the needs of program and evaluation beneficiaries in poverty, those who are otherwise disadvantaged, and those from other backgrounds and cultures. Educational and social service providers as well as evaluators must be responsive to stakeholders who bring their own unique parts of the world with them (Guzman, 2003; Hood, 2004). However, the JCSEE and the revision task force recognize the impossibility of building ANSI standards that adequately reflect the diversity of linguistic, political, and cultural perspectives worldwide. The third edition will remain a consensus document of North American evaluators and those who interact with and provide feedback to the JCSEE. Evaluators with extensive international, cross-cultural, and multicultural experience will contribute to and strengthen this edition, but these contributions will not make it a set of international standards.

Proposed Framework for an Evaluation of the *Program Evaluation Standards*. Historically, in the development cycles for JCSEE evaluation standards, evaluation of all aspects of the standards books has been ongoing and has included formative reviews and evaluations (expert critiques, national and international reviews, national hearings, field trials) and final expert summative judgments by the membership of the JCSEE as they integrate all of the formative information (JCSEE, 1981, 1994; Sanders, 1994). As the current task force, we have built on these experiences to craft its framework for evaluating the second edition of *Program Evaluation Standards* (Sanders and Vogel, 1987; Piontek and Torres, 1992; Yarbrough, 2002) as a first step in the process leading to the next revision.

Evaluation is a self-referential activity (Shadish, Cook, and Leviton, 1991; Scriven, 2003; Alkin, 2004). Since the *Program Evaluation Standards* can be used for evaluating educational media, products, and materials, it has relevance for its own evaluation. We have every right to expect the *Program Evaluation Standards* itself to further the evaluation qualities of utility, feasibility, propriety, and accuracy. One strand of any evaluation of the *Program Evaluation Standards* focuses on the extent to which the publication itself furthers high-quality evaluation scholarship and practice.

We are conceptualizing a framework for evaluating the second edition of *Program Evaluation Standards* preliminary to a third edition that will provide information about the following questions:

1. Who are the primary users of the second edition of *Program Evaluation Standards*, and what do their demographics reveal about the relevance and transferability of the standards to different situations and applications?
2. To what extent has the *Program Evaluation Standards* met its espoused purposes and uses, and how could it meet these more efficiently and effectively?
3. What additional reasonable uses should be under consideration for the *Program Evaluation Standards* in the next revision?
4. What features, standards, or components need to be added, maintained as is, improved, deleted, or radically changed in the next edition?
5. To what extent is the *Program Evaluation Standards* congruent with current scholarship on and best practices of program evaluation? How could it be made more in line with best practices and scholarship?
6. How useful is the current *Program Evaluation Standards* to practicing evaluators and evaluation stakeholders, and how can it be made more useful?
7. How complementary are the Program Evaluation Standards with other evaluation standards, other professional standards, and other guiding principles, including those of the JCSEE sponsoring organizations, other professional organizations, and other evaluation associations, both national and international? What can be learned of value from discussions in other countries and on other continents about adaptations and uses of the standards in those locations?
8. What are the most important and most widespread instrumental, conceptual (enlightenment), and process uses of the *Program Evaluation Standards?* How can the capacity for effective and efficient use for intended users be improved?

We anticipate information to address these questions from surveys of the membership of the JCSEE-sponsoring organizations and other evaluation stakeholders; interviews with targeted samples of evaluation practitioners, professional evaluation organizations and businesses, and leading evaluation theorists and researchers; reviews of evaluation scholarship; and open calls for feedback from national and international program evaluators.

Because the *Program Evaluation Standards* evaluation and revision process is just beginning, information addressing some of the questions we have set out is only beginning to be available. Nevertheless, a few comments based on preliminary literature reviews and survey responses are possible.

Uses Made of the *Program Evaluation Standards*. The "Functional Table of Contents" of the second edition lists the uses related to specific evaluation tasks, such as deciding whether to evaluate, defining the evaluation problem, designing the evaluation, and other tasks necessary for implementing the evaluation project. The standard statements as well as the cases and other supporting sections highlight other critical uses of the standards, including helping clients and sponsors select evaluators, supporting the training and development of evaluation students and practicing evaluators, and helping stakeholders and others evaluate evaluations (metaevaluation). Numerous sources convey the extensive uses made of the *Program Evaluation Standards* in the past twenty years.

One source of information about the utility of the Program Evaluation Standards is the extent to which practicing evaluators are familiar with and use them. Numerous reported evaluations (Renger, Passons, and Cimetta, 2003; Scott-Little, Hamann, and Jurs, 2002) acknowledge use of the standards to guide their projects. In recent years, the *American Journal of Evaluation* has published metaevaluations that have relied on the *Program Evaluation Standards*. Stufflebeam (2003) has developed extensive checklists for using the *Program Evaluation Standards* for such purposes. While numerous professional organizations have sponsored the *Program Evaluation Standards* and its development, none to date has endorsed the *Program Evaluation Standards* for its membership. However, at least one division of a large professional organization has encouraged its membership to use the *Program Evaluation Standards*. In the call for proposals for the 2005 annual meeting, American Educational Research Association Division H mandated that program evaluation proposals for presentation explicitly address the *Program Evaluation Standards*.

Conceptual Congruence and Contributions. During development of the second edition of *Program Evaluation Standards,* extensive reviews of the literature informed the writing of all sections. For the utility standards, one JCSEE member documented in thorough detail the literature on evaluation use and how it formed the background for the conceptualization of the utility standards and their supporting cases and other material (Thompson, 1994). Similar congruence in other areas (feasibility, propriety, and accuracy) was a goal during this development phase.

A key question facing the current review process is how best to investigate the current congruence of the *Program Evaluation Standards* given the increasing body of scholarship addressing each of these areas. Since 1994, there have been extensive developments related to stakeholder empowerment (Fetterman, 2001), responsive evaluation (Stake, 2004), collaborative and participatory evaluation (Greene, 2002; King, 1998, 2004; Cousins and Whitmore, 1998), democratic processes (Henry and Mark, 2003), organizational learning (Torres and Preskill, 2001), cultural competence (Guzman, 2003; Thompson-Robinson, Hopson, and SenGupta, 2004), program theory (Chen, 1990; Rossi, Lipsey, and Freeman, 2004; Donaldson, 2003; SenGupta, 2002), and social justice (House and Howe, 1999), to name a few. The revision process leading to a third edition will need to develop extensive lists of potential supporting documentation and pay attention to both breadth and depth in expanding the supporting documentation and conceptual foundation of the standards.

Several widely used books on evaluation have explicitly incorporated the *Program Evaluation Standards* in their conceptual structure (Fitzpatrick, Sanders, and Worthen, 2004; Rossi, Lipsey, and Freeman, 2004; Patton, 1997; Stake, 2004) and indicated how the standards have contributed to thinking about program evaluation as well as the practice of program evaluation. Stufflebeam (2001) used the Program Evaluation Standards to frame a metaevaluation of program evaluation approaches in order to reach his own expert judgment about which approaches are appropriate foundation models for program evaluation practice in the twenty-first century.

Uses of the *Program Evaluation Standards* in an International Perspective. The processes followed in the development of the second edition of *Program Evaluation Standards* were oriented to and guided by ANSI-approved procedures. As ANSI procedures, the second edition took on specific valuable roles in North America (Stufflebeam, 2004). The JCSEE procedures and products have enabled extensive deliberations of how standards might be created, developed, and modified by various groups and organizations in and outside the United States. All who use or develop standards must contend with the questions of how specific to make evaluation standards, how rigorous a fit between standards and practice to endorse, and the extent to which standards should simply relate exemplars of evaluation practice (a descriptive perspective), codify observed best practice (a normative perspective), or be used to suggest how to practice best (a prescriptive perspective). This fine line is easily overlooked. As long as one uses the *Program Evaluation Standards* with the understanding that the standards are illustrative, potentially exemplary, and not adequate for detailed prescription, then their usefulness may be extended.

In its attempt to incorporate best knowledge and approaches to program evaluation from the best theory, research, and practice, the JCSEE has produced a discussion document to inspire individual American and Canadian evaluations and to inform general practice and conceptual discussions about program evaluation. The second edition of *Program Evaluation Standards* was never intended as a specific prescriptive set of standards that could be followed as a recipe for competent evaluation (JCSEE, 1981, 1994). Its founding chair articulated this long-standing perspective of the JCSEE: "I think it is up to every evaluation group to decide whether or not they want evaluation standards and, if so, to proceed as systematically and professionally as they can. Certainly, groups that want standards should make their own decisions about what the standards should be. And, of course, standard-setting bodies should regularly subject their standards to evaluation, improvement, and independent confirmation of their value to constituents" (Stufflebeam, 2004, p. 102).

However, although they are fundamentally North American, developed and used primarily in the United States and Canada, the *Program Evaluation*

Standards has found application outside the United States (Russon, 2000). In response to initiatives outside the JCSEE's purview, the second edition has been translated into several languages for use in other countries (Beywl, 2000) and has led to modified standards in several countries, including Switzerland (Widmer, Landert, and Bacmann, 2000), as well as for use in Africa (Hood, 2004). Countless evaluators who speak English as their second language have read the *Program Evaluation Standards* and been informed about the field of program evaluation, applying these standards with modifications in their countries and cultures. In addition, if current trends continue, other future evaluation societies yet to be founded around the world will find inspiration in the Program Evaluation Standards and the procedures the JCSEE used to develop them in order to develop their own program evaluation standards.

Increasing numbers of evaluators and scholars are likely to apply and evaluate the Program Evaluation Standards in other locations outside the United States (Jang, 2000). For example, Marino and Fischer (2003) reviewed the work of evaluators and professional evaluation groups in Brazil compared to the Program Evaluation Standards and, based on numerous case studies, recommended Program Evaluation Standards use in Brazil with slight modifications and clarifications. After using the standards to meta-evaluate selected evaluations in Bangladesh, Chatterji (forthcoming) was generally positive about three areas (utility, accuracy, and feasibility), but concluded that the propriety standards might need revision to be most effective in that context. Propriety appears to be a problematic area for international applications, as several writers have previously demonstrated (Russon, 2000; Smith, Chircop, and Mukherjee, 2000; Jang, 2000).

It is the current position of the JCSEE Revision Task Force that all attempts to use the Program Evaluation Standards outside the United States provide valuable information about how the standards might be improved to work better in the United States with diverse cultural and ethnic groups. Diversity in the United States mirrors in a microcosm the diversity of the world at large. Attempts to adapt the standards for use in international situations and locales as well as the procedures of other groups to develop standards and the standards that they develop can provide insight into ways to improve future revisions of the *Program Evaluation Standards*. As ANSI standards, the JCSEE, however, are dependent on consensus procedures that emphasize heavily those with a connection to North American institutions.

Conclusion

It would be a gross distortion to conclude from this brief history that evaluation as a practice field or as a theoretical area for disciplined inquiry is uniquely or even primarily North American. Current understandings of evaluation have their philosophical roots in diverse sources, from the works of Greek philosophers laying out the foundations of value theory, to the

British empiricists and German rationalists, to more recent works influencing conceptions of social justice (Rawls, 1971). Similarly, investigations of the nature of evaluation and judgment from a psychological and social psychological perspective rest on the works of European psychological traditions and are informed by studies around the globe.

However, what was of historical note in the development of the JCSEE *Program Evaluation Standards* is the dramatic turn to socially innovative programs in a climate of optimism tempered by accountability systems in the 1960s and 1970s in the United States. The demand for program evaluations escalated overnight without the existence of much practice literature or specific expertise. Those in need of program evaluators had to turn to the large body of social science researchers schooled in techniques from educational, psychological, sociological, anthropological, historical, and economic research. In retrospect, it is easy to see how these researchers, highly trained in specific investigatory paradigms, were constrained by this same training. Many evaluators were guided primarily by existing methodological approaches and constructed questions that were congruent with their understanding of social science scholarship and that were answerable by the method of choice. In modern evaluation, identification of the important questions is more likely to precede decisions about method and the specification of measurement units (Shulha and Wilson, 2003). A modern evaluation approach requires that intended users' questions inform the choice of methodology in order to make an efficient, effective, and useful evaluation more likely.

In approaching this third revision, we are aware that much about program evaluation and its practice in the United States is also foundational for other countries and locations. When the original Program Evaluation Standards were developed, bringing the diverse program evaluation voices from the North American venue under one tent was surely a formidable task. Developing standards that would facilitate useful, feasible, proper, and accurate evaluations serving the widely discrepant voices of program evaluation practitioners, theorists, and stakeholders in the United States has consistently been a primary focus of the JCSEE (Stufflebeam, 2004). With regard to the third revision, our goal is to continue this tradition and to attend to all suggestions for maintenance, enhancement, and improvement of *The Program Evaluation Standards* from all users and stakeholders, both national and international, in accordance with ANSI procedures.

References

Alkin, M. C. "Comparing Evaluation Points of View." In M. C. Alkin (ed.), *Evaluation Roots: Tracing Theorists' Views and Influences.* Thousand Oaks, Calif.: Sage, 2004.

Beywl, W. "Standards for Evaluation: On the Way to Guiding Principles in German Evaluation." In C. Russon (ed.), *The Program Evaluation Standards in International Settings.* Kalamazoo: Evaluation Center, Western Michigan University, 2000.

Chatterji, M. "Applying the Joint Committee's 1994 Standards in International Contexts: A Case Study of Education Evaluations in Bangladesh." *Teachers College Record,* forthcoming.

Chen, H. T. *Theory-Driven Evaluations.* Thousand Oaks, Calif.: Sage, 1990.

Cousins, J. B., and Whitmore, E. "Framing Participatory Evaluation." In E. Whitmore (ed.), *Understanding and Practicing Participatory Evaluation.* New Directions for Evaluation, no. 80. San Francisco: Jossey-Bass, 1998.

Cronbach, L. J. "Coefficient Alpha and the Internal Structure of Tests." *Psychometrika,* 1951, no. 16, 297–334.

Cronbach, L. J. *Educational Program and Research Design.* San Francisco: Jossey-Bass, 1982.

de Tocqueville, A. *Democracy in America.* New York: Penguin, 2004.

Donaldson, S. I. "Theory-Driven Evaluation in the New Millennium." In S. I. Donaldson and M. Scriven (eds.), *Evaluating Social Programs and Problems.* Mahwah, N.J.: Erlbaum, 2003.

Feldt, L. S., and Brennan, R. L. "Reliability." In R. L. Linn (ed.), *Educational Measurement.* (3rd ed.) Phoenix, Ariz.: American Council on Education and the Oryx Press, 1993.

Fetterman, D. M. *Foundations of Empowerment Evaluation.* Thousand Oaks, Calif.: Sage, 2001.

Fitzpatrick, J. L., Sanders, J. R., and Worthen, B. R. *Program Evaluation: Alternative Approaches and Practical Guidelines.* (3rd ed.) White Plains, N.Y.: Longman, 2004.

Greene, J. "With a Splash of Soda, Please: Towards Active Engagement with Difference." *Evaluation,* 2002, *8,* 259–266.

Guba, E. G., and Lincoln, Y. S. *Fourth Generation Evaluation.* Thousand Oaks, Calif.: Sage, 1989.

Guzman, B. L. "Examining the Role of Cultural Competency in Program Evaluation: Visions for New Millennium Evaluators." In S. I. Donaldson and M. Scriven (eds.), *Evaluating Social Programs and Problems.* Mahwah, N.J.: Erlbaum, 2003.

Henry, G. T., and Mark, M. M. "Beyond Use: Understanding Evaluation's Influence on Attitudes and Actions." *American Journal of Evaluation,* 2003, *24,* 293–314.

Hergenhahn, B. R. *An Introduction to the History of Psychology.* (4th ed.) Belmont, Calif.: Wadsworth, 2001.

Hood, S. "A Journey to Understand the Role of Culture in Program Evaluation: Snapshots and Personal Reflections of One African American evaluator." In M. Thompson-Robinson, R. Hopson, and S. SenGupta (eds.), *In Search of Cultural Competence in Evaluation.* New Directions for Evaluation, no. 102. San Francisco: Jossey Bass, 2004.

House, E. R., and Howe, K. R. *Values in Evaluation and Social Research.* Thousand Oaks, Calif.: Sage, 1999.

Jang, S. "The Appropriateness of Joint Committee Standards in Non-Western Settings: A Case Study of South Korea." In C. Russon (ed.), *The Program Evaluation Standards in International Settings.* Kalamazoo, Mich.: Evaluation Center, Western Michigan University, 2000.

Joint Committee on Standards for Educational Evaluation. *Standards for Evaluations of Educational Programs, Projects, and Materials.* New York: McGraw-Hill, 1981.

Joint Committee on Standards for Educational Evaluation. *Personnel Evaluation Standards.* Thousand Oaks, Calif.: Sage, 1988.

Joint Committee on Standards for Educational Evaluation. *Program Evaluation Standards.* (2nd ed.) Thousand Oaks, Calif.: Sage, 1994.

Joint Committee on Standards for Educational Evaluation. *Student Evaluation Standards.* Thousand Oaks, Calif.: Corwin, 2003.

King, J. A. "Making Sense of Participatory Evaluation Practice." In E. Whitmore (ed.), *Understanding and Practicing Participatory Evaluation.* New Directions for Evaluation, no. 80. San Francisco: Jossey-Bass, 1998.

King, J. A. "Evaluating Educational Programs and Projects in the United States." In T. Kellaghan and D. L. Stufflebeam (eds.), *International Handbook on Educational Evaluation.* Norwood, Mass.: Kluwer, 2003.

King, J. A. "The Roots of Participatory Evaluation." In M. C. Alkin (ed.), *Evaluation Roots: Tracing Theorists' Views and Influences.* Thousand Oaks, Calif.: Sage, 2004.

Marino, E., and Fischer, R. M. "Applicability of the Joint Committee Program Evaluation Standards in Brazil." Paper presented at the annual meeting of the American Evaluation Society, Reno, Nev., 2003.

Mark, M. M., Henry, G. T., and Julnes, G. *Evaluation: An Integrated Framework for Understanding, Guiding, and Improving Policies and Programs.* San Francisco: Jossey-Bass, 2000.

Patton, M. Q. *Utilization-Focused Evaluation.* (3rd ed.) Thousand Oaks, Calif.: Sage, 1997.

Piontek, M. E., and Torres, R. T. "Field Test Report for August 1992 Draft of Program Evaluation Standards." Kalamazoo: Evaluation Center, Western Michigan University, 1992.

Rawls, J. *A Theory of Justice.* Cambridge, Mass.: Belknap Press, 1971.

Renger, R., Passons, O., and Cimetta, A. "Evaluating Housing Revitalization Projects: Critical Lessons for All Evaluators." *American Journal of Evaluation,* 2003, 24(1), 51–64.

Rossi, P. H. (ed.). *Standards for Evaluation Practice.* New Directions for Program Evaluation, no. 15. San Francisco: Jossey-Bass, 1982.

Rossi, P. H., Lipsey, M. W., and Freeman, H. E. *Evaluation: A Systematic Approach.* (7th ed.) Thousand Oaks, Calif.: Sage, 2004.

Rossi, P., and Freeman, H. *Evaluation: A Systematic Approach.* (2nd ed.) Thousand Oaks, Calif.: Sage, 1982.

Russon, C. "The Program Evaluation Standards in International Settings." Kalamazoo: Evaluation Center, Western Michigan University, 2000.

Russon, C. "Foreword." In C. Russon (ed.), The *Program Evaluation Standards in International Settings.* Kalamazoo: Evaluation Center, Western Michigan University, 2000.

Sanders, J. R. "The Process of Developing National Standards That Meet ANSI Guidelines." *Journal of Experimental Education,* 1994, 63(1), 5–12.

Sanders, J. R., and Vogel, S. M. "Field Test Report for the Second Draft of Standards for Evaluations of Educational Personnel." Kalamazoo: Evaluation Center, Western Michigan University, 1987.

Scott-Little, C., Hamann, M. S., and Jurs, S. G. "Evaluations of After-School Programs: A Meta-Evaluation of Methodologies and Narrative Synthesis of Findings." *American Journal of Evaluation,* 2002, 23, 387–419.

Scriven, M. "The Methodology of Evaluation." In R. W. Tyler, R. M. Gagne, and M. Scriven (eds.), *Perspectives of Curriculum Evaluation.* Skokie, Ill.: Rand McNally, 1967.

Scriven, M. "Evaluation in the New Millennium: The Transdisciplinary Vision." In S. I. Donaldson and M. Scriven (eds.), *Evaluating Social Programs and Problems.* Mahwah, N.J.: Erlbaum, 2003.

SenGupta, S. "Commentary: Begin with a Good Program Theory: The Case of the Missing Guiding Principle." *American Journal of Evaluation,* 2002, 23(1), 103–106.

SenGupta, S., Hopson, R., and Thompson-Robinson, M. "Cultural Competence in Evaluation: An Overview." In M. Thompson-Robinson, R. Hopson, and S. SenGupta (eds.), *In Search of Cultural Competence in Evaluation.* New Directions for Evaluation, no. 102. San Francisco: Jossey-Bass, 2004.

Shadish, W. R., Cook, T. D., and Leviton, L. C. *Foundations of Program Evaluation: Theories of Practice.* Newbury Park, Calif.: Sage, 1991.

Shulha, L. M., and Wilson, R. J. "Collaborative Mixed-Method Research." In A. Tashakkori and C. Teddlie (eds.), *Handbook of Mixed Methodology.* Thousand Oaks, Calif.: Sage, 2003.

Smith, N. L., Chircop, S., and Mukherjee, P. "Considerations on the Development of Culturally Relevant Evaluation Standards." In C. Russon (ed.), The *Program*

   Evaluation Standards in International Settings. Kalamazoo: Evaluation Center, Western Michigan University, 2000.

Stake, R. *Standards-Based and Responsive Evaluation.* Thousand Oaks, Calif.: Sage, 2004.

Stufflebeam, D. L. "The Use and Abuse of Evaluation in Title III." *Theory into Practice,* 1967, no. 6, 126–133.

Stufflebeam, D. L. (ed.). *Evaluation Models.* New Directions for Evaluation, no. 89. San Francisco: Jossey-Bass, 2001.

Stufflebeam, D. L. "Professional Standards and Principles for Evaluations." In T. Kellaghan and D. L. Stufflebeam (eds.), *International Handbook of Educational Evaluation.* Norwell, Mass.: Kluwer, 2003.

Stufflebeam, D. L. "A Note on the Purposes, Development, and Applicability of the Joint Committee Evaluation Standards." *American Journal of Evaluation,* 2004, 25(1), 99–102.

Stufflebeam, D. L. "The Twenty-First Century CIPP Model: Origins, Development, and Use." In M. C. Alkin (ed.), *Evaluation Roots: Tracing Theorists' Views and Influences.* Thousand Oaks, Calif.: Sage, 2004.

Thompson, B. "The Revised Program Evaluation Standards and Their Correlation with the Evaluation Use Literature." *Journal of Experimental Education,* 1994, 63(1), 54–81.

Thompson-Robinson, M., Hopson, R., and SenGupta, S. (eds.). *In Search of Cultural Competence in Evaluation.* New Directions for Evaluation, no. 102. San Francisco: Jossey-Bass, 2004.

Torres, R. T., and Preskill, H. "Evaluation and Organizational Learning: Past, Present, and Future." *American Journal of Evaluation,* 2001, 22, 387–395.

Tyler, R. W. "General Statement on Evaluation." *Journal of Educational Research,* 1942, no. 36, 492–501.

Weiss, C. H. *Evaluation Research: Methods of Assessing Program Effectiveness.* Upper Saddle River, N.J.: Prentice Hall, 1972.

Weiss, C. H. *Evaluation: Methods for Studying Programs and Policies.* (2nd ed.) Upper Saddle River, N.J.: Prentice Hall, 1998.

Widmer, T., Landert, C., and Bacmann, N. "Evaluation Standards Recommended by the Swiss Evaluation Society (SEVAL)." In C. Russon (ed.), The *Program Evaluation Standards in International Settings.* Kalamazoo: Evaluation Center, Western Michigan University, 2000.

Worthen, B. R., and Sanders, J. R. *Educational Evaluation: Alternative Approaches and Practical Guidelines.* White Plains, N.Y.: Longman, 1987.

Worthen, B. R., Sanders, J. R., and Fitzpatrick, J. L. *Program Evaluation: Alternative Approaches and Practical Guidelines.* (2nd ed.) White Plains, N.Y.: Longman, 1997.

Yarbrough, D. B. "Theoretical and Practical Considerations in Evaluating the Student Evaluation Standards." Paper presented at the annual meeting of the National Council on Measurement in Education, New Orleans, La., 2002.

DONALD B. YARBROUGH is director of the Center for Evaluation and Assessment and associate professor in the Department of Psychological and Quantitative Foundations, University of Iowa, Iowa City.

LYN M. SHULHA is associate professor and director of the Assessment and Evaluation Group, Faculty of Education, Queen's University at Kingston, Canada.

FLORA CARUTHERS is staff director in the Office of Program Policy Analysis and Government Accountability, Tallahassee, Florida.

3

The author presents standards developments in the
national evaluation organizations of Switzerland,
Germany, France, and the United Kingdom, as well as
related work in the European Commission.

The Development and Status of Evaluation Standards in Western Europe

Thomas Widmer

For many years, the European evaluation community did not recognize eval-uation standards as a relevant tool for quality assurance. References to the developments in the United States were exceptionally rare in the European evaluation literature during the 1970s and 1980s. One of the first articles on evaluation standards to appear in the European literature was Wolfgang Beywl's discussion (1988) of the Evaluation Standards of the Evaluation Research Society (ERS; Evaluation Research Society Standards Committee, 1982) and the Standards for Educational Evaluation (Joint Committee on Standards for Educational Evaluation, 1981). Another early example of the standards discussion in Europe was the translation of the ERS Standards into German (Koch and Wittmann, 1990; Kistler and Becker, 1990).

In the past decade, however, discussion about evaluation standards has accelerated in Europe. Based on the cultural diversity of the region, national evaluation organizations have taken distinct approaches to activities in the field of quality assurance in evaluation (Toulemonde, 2000). This chapter examines the domain of evaluation standards since the beginning of the 1990s in Western Europe. It looks specifically at Switzerland, Germany, France, and the United Kingdom because they are the European front-runners in this domain.

Thanks to the members of the Working Group on Standards, Guidelines, and Ethical Codes in Evaluation of the European Evaluation Society for sharing their experiences.

Although the focus of this contribution is on evaluation standards, it also discusses documents with other labels, specifically principles and charters. The argument underlying this decision is twofold. First, despite their names, these documents play similar roles as nominal evaluation standards. Second, in my view, their existence has an unavoidable relevance for the future of evaluation standards in Europe.

Switzerland

Evaluation writers have not identified Switzerland as one of the front-runners in European evaluation (Horber-Papazian and Thévoz, 1990; Bussmann, 1995, 1996; Spinatsch, 2002; Derlien and Rist, 2002; Leeuw, 2004; Widmer and Neuenschwander, forthcoming). Although many view it generally as more of a laggard than a leader, the activities initialized by a Committee of the Swiss Federation in launching a national research program that provided funds for evaluation research projects boosted the development of the Swiss evaluation community in the late 1980s and early 1990s. Quality concerns were a central focus of the research program, and for the first time, evaluation standards were applied within this framework in two metaevaluative projects (Widmer, 1996; Widmer, Rothmayr, and Serdült, 1996). For these metaevaluations, standards from the first edition of the Joint Committee Standards (1981) were systematically used as criteria to assess the quality of fifteen Swiss evaluation studies from the policy domains of the environment, industry, energy, social policy, and foreign policy. The results demonstrated the general applicability of the Joint Committee standards in the Swiss context as well as in fields outside education. However, the studies also recommended some minor revisions of U.S.-Canadian standards, such as merging several related standards and reducing the total number of standards (Widmer, 2000).

As one of the first activities of the Swiss Evaluation Society (Schweizerische Evaluationsgesellschaft/Société Suisse d'évaluation/Società Svizzera di valutazione, SEVAL), founded in 1996, the board decided to establish a working group covering the issues of quality and standards. After a broad discussion, the working group, which consisted of representatives from evaluation practice, administration, and research, made two decisions: that SEVAL should establish its own evaluation standards and that these standards should rely on the second edition of the Joint Committee Program Standards (Joint Committee, 1994). There were several revisions made in a multilingual setting within the working group and among SEVAL membership, leading to a first version of the standards in 1999. The general assembly approved the Evaluation Standards of SEVAL (SEVAL Standards; Widmer, Landert, and Bachmann, 2000) in spring 2001. With the approval, SEVAL acted as a pioneer, becoming the first European evaluation society (and the first outside the United States and Canada) to establish its own evaluation standards.

The SEVAL Standards is a twenty-page document that consists of twenty-seven standards, available in German, French, and English (see www.seval.ch). These standards follow the general structure of the Joint Committee with the four categories of utility, feasibility, propriety, and accuracy. In contrast to the American standards, the SEVAL Standards completely omit one standard, Service Orientation, and add Clarifying the Objectives of the Evaluation. In addition, some standards are consolidated while others are revised or reformulated.

Since their creation, evaluators have applied the SEVAL Standards in various settings, and the standards are well known among SEVAL membership, which currently numbers more than three hundred members. (In relation to the small Swiss population of 7.3 million, this represents a high degree of participation; the same proportion for the United States would mean that American Evaluation Association would have roughly 11,400 members.) Non-SEVAL members are also involved in evaluation activities, especially in commissioning evaluations. Initially, the SEVAL Standards were used in formative and summative metaevaluations. Now they are also used in advice for evaluation practice, for quality assurance purposes, and as teaching aids for evaluation education. In general, the Swiss evaluation community appears to maintain a strong acceptance of the SEVAL Standards. However, depending on the degree of professionalization of the evaluation function, differences among fields of application exist (Läubli Loud, 2004; Widmer, 2004a, forthcoming).

Germany

Like Switzerland, Germany has not been known as a prominent nation in European evaluation, although it also experienced increased activities in the evaluation domain in the 1990s (Derlien, 2002; Stockmann, 2004). Influenced by the Swiss achievements and by the translation of the Joint Committee Program Evaluation Standards into German, the German Evaluation Society (Deutsche Gesellschaft für Evaluation, DeGEval) started a standards-setting process in 2000 (Joint Committee, 2000). After a survey among the membership and a decision by the general assembly, a standards committee was established. The committee chose the Joint Committee Program Evaluation Standards and the SEVAL Standards as starting points. In fall 2001, the general assembly of DeGEval formally adopted the DeGEval Standards that the committee developed.

The DeGEval Standards is a fifty-page document that includes a summary in English (see www.degeval.de). Similar to the SEVAL Standards, it focuses on the four broad categories of the Joint Committee standards: utility, feasibility, propriety or fairness, and accuracy. DeGEval followed the revisions made in the SEVAL Standards; however, DeGEval also introduced changes. These changes included the consolidation of the conflict of interest and the neutral reporting standards into a new standard about unbiased conduct and reporting (Beywl, 2000; Beywl and Taut, 2000).

After the adoption of the DeGEval Standards, two issues became controversial within DeGEval. The first involved the role of society in the application of the standards, especially the question of whether DeGEval itself should conduct metaevaluations applying the standards. The DeGEval decided that society will support the application of standards but will not conduct metaevaluations itself. The second issue questioned the need for specific standards for self-evaluations. Although a draft set of standards for self-evaluations has been drafted (see Chapter Four, this issue), this discussion is ongoing (see Müller-Kohlenberg and Beywl, 2003). Overall, however, the general utility of the DeGEval Standards is not challenged, although some criticisms have been articulated for specific fields of application. Schwab (2003), for example, argues that the application of standards is restricted if no evaluation culture exists, as in the field of structural policy in Germany.

France

The history of evaluation in France contains many successes and failures (Fontaine and Monnier, 2002), a statement that applies equally well to discussions in the standards domain. In the early 1990s, the Scientific Evaluation Council (Conseil scientifique de l'évaluation) applied a set of standards that it had developed to assess the quality of evaluation practices (Conseil scientifique de l'évaluation, 1996). This council was dissolved in 1998 and was replaced by the National Evaluation Council (Conseil national de l'évaluation). To my knowledge, the National Evaluation Council has not conducted any activities in the standards domain (Barbier, 2003). Instead, the French Evaluation Society (Société française d'évaluation, SFE), established in 1999, launched a process for developing what it called a charter. The SFE's Working Group on Standards and Ethics took into consideration the work done in other countries. After a lengthy discussion, they decided against following the developments in other countries, choosing instead to create a generic document (Barbier and Perret, 2000). In fall 2003, SFE's general assembly adopted the Charter of Evaluation Guiding Principles for Public Policies and Programs (SFE Charter, 2003).

The SFE Charter, a two-page document available in French and English (respectively, www.sfe.asso.fr/pdf/charte.pdf and http://www.sfe.asso.fr/pdf/charte-english.pdf), consists of a preamble and six guiding principles: pluralism, independence, competence, respecting the integrity of individuals, transparency, and responsibility. Every principle is briefly described in the document. The working group is currently disseminating the charter to its members on behalf of SFE. Given its recent creation, the time line is too short to assess the use or acceptance of the document within the French evaluation community.

United Kingdom

In contrast to Switzerland, Germany, and France, the United Kingdom has a longer tradition in evaluation and belongs to the group of European countries that launched an evaluation function early on (Jenkins and Gray, 1990; Gray and Jenkins, 2002). Evaluation rapidly reached a relatively high level of institutionalization in the United Kingdom, including the U.K. Evaluation Society (UKES), founded in 1994. A long-standing tradition of exchange exists between British evaluators with the American and Commonwealth evaluation communities. However, the U.K. evaluation community has generally ignored the issue of standards, guidelines, and principles. Finally, in 2003, the UKES presented good practice guidelines that a committee of the society developed.

The "Guidelines for Good Practice in Evaluation of the UKES" (United Kingdom Evaluation Society, n.d.) is a six-page document. It consists of separate guidelines for evaluators (nineteen guidelines), for commissioners (eighteen guidelines), for evaluation participants (seven guidelines), and for self-evaluation (seventeen guidelines). Every guideline circumscribes good practice of one of the groups mentioned and is presented in one sentence. A short preface explains the role, function, and relevance of the guidelines, especially emphasizing the evolving nature of the document. Since these guidelines have existed for only a short period, no information about the application of the standards in evaluation practice is yet available.

European Commission

Within the European Commission (EC), a varied practice of evaluation has evolved in the different EC units in the past decade (Summa and Toulemonde, 2002; Williams, de Laat, and Stern, 2002; Leeuw, 2004). In some cases, good practice guidelines, principles, or similar documents inform evaluation practice. For example, the MEANS (Methods for Evaluating Structural Policies) collection was developed to support the evaluation of socioeconomic programs within European structural policy (EC Structural Funds, 1999). In order to have more coherent evaluation policies in the various units of the EC, an evaluation network was established. Coordinated by the Directorate General for Budget, this network consists of people involved in evaluation activities throughout the commission. Evaluation quality is one of the issues regularly discussed in this context. Together with the strategic planning and programming network, a working party created the standards regarded as necessary for development of the evaluation system. At the end of 2002, the process ended with the presentation of Evaluation Standards and Good Practice, which were implemented in July 2003.

The EC Evaluation Standards and Good Practice (EC Standards and Practice) is a twenty-four-page document (see europa.eu.int/comm/

budget/evaluation/index_en.htm) that contains quality standards and good practice. Standards and good practice are organized in the following groups: profile, role, task, and resources of the evaluation function (eight standards); management of evaluation activities (thirteen standards); evaluation process (twelve standards); and quality of reports (six standards). The main distinction between standards and good practice lies in the fact that the standards are binding, in contrast to the supporting characteristics of the good practices.

The EC Standards and Good Practice appear in the core of an evaluation guide published in November 2003 (EC Directorate General for Budget, 2003). This document explains the standards and good practice more broadly in order to assist those involved in or responsible for the evaluation function within the EC. Since both the EC Standards and Practice and the related evaluation guide have only recently been presented, no information is yet available about experiences with them in evaluation practice.

European Standards and the Program Evaluation Standards: A Comparison

The different standards, guidelines, and similar documents show a high degree of variation. Table 3.1 emphasizes some of these dimensions in the design of standards in Europe. For comparative reasons, the table also includes the North American Joint Committee Program Evaluation Standards. As the table shows, in a broad sense, there are clear similarities as well as differences among the six sets of standards:

• *Relationship to the Joint Committee Program Evaluation Standards.* Unlike the Joint Committee standards, which address educational programs exclusively, all European standards are more generally applicable and not directed to a specific field. Because the JCS formed the basis for the development of the SEVAL and DeGEval documents, the similarities they share with the Joint Committee standards are, not surprisingly, much higher than in the other documents. Like the JCS, the SEVAL and DeGEval exclude personnel evaluation; in addition, DeGEval partially includes self-evaluation, which is not addressed by the JCS. The EC Standards and Practice and the Joint Committee standards include or exclude certain types of evaluation objects. For example, EC excludes a certain type of evaluation (evaluations of individual projects funded under programs), whereas the Joint Committee standards include evaluation of educational programs, projects, and materials. The SFE Charter and the UKES guidelines cover a broad scope of evaluation types. The Joint Committee standards are defined by inclusion of evaluation types (educational programs) and by exclusion (personnel and student evaluations).

• *Similarities.* The European evaluation organizations have demonstrated a high degree of activities in the field of standard setting in the past

Table 3.1. Comparison of Select Standards in Europe and the Joint Committee Standards

Dimensions	SEVAL Standards	DeGEval Standards	SFE Charter	UKES Guidelines	EC Standards and Practice	JC Standards
Sponsoring body	National evaluation society	National evaluation society	National evaluation society	National evaluation society	European Commission	North American associations
Regulated object	Evaluation (process and product)	Evaluation (process and product)	Evaluation (process and product)	Parties involved in evaluation	EC bodies involved in evaluation	Evaluation (process and product)
Who is addressed	Parties involved in evaluation	Parties involved in evaluation	SFE membership	Parties involved in evaluation differentiated by their roles	EC bodies involved in evaluation	Parties involved in evaluation
Issue date (1st ed.)	2000 (1999)	2001	2003	2003	2002	1994 (1981)
Level of specificity (level of detail)	High	High	Low	Medium	Medium	High
Geographical scope	Switzerland	Germany and Austria	France	United Kingdom	Europe	North America
Evaluation fields	All fields	All fields	Evaluation of public activities	All fields	Evaluation in all EC departments	Education and training
Evaluation types	All types, excluding personnel evaluations	All types, excluding personnel evaluations and (partially) self-evaluations	All types	All types	Excluding evaluations of individual projects funded under programs	All evaluations of programs, projects, and materials, excluding personnel evaluations
Functionality (uses)	Ensuring and promoting quality in evaluation	Safeguarding and developing quality of evaluation and promoting public and professional dialogue about evaluation	Expression of values shared by SFE membership	Starting point for deliberation and as reference for statements of ethics, intentions, and generic practice	Improving the coherence and quality of evaluation in the European Commission	Framework for designing and assessing evaluations
Nature	Describing best practice (maximal standards)	Describing best practice (maximal standards)	Platform for establishing common values	Informing about good (honorable and effective) practice	Minimal standards and good practice	Describing best practice (maximal standards)
Status	Not binding	Not binding	Not binding	Not binding	Partially binding	Not binding

several years. With the exception of the EC document, national evaluation societies sponsored the European documents, which therefore have a national scope. With the exception of standards within the EC Standards and Practice, the standards are not binding.

• *Differences.* Whereas the other documents focus on the evaluation itself, the UKES Guidelines and the EC Standards and Practice provide guidelines (that is, codes of conduct) for the behavior of individuals or groups. Although all stakeholders involved in the evaluation process are addressed in these documents, the audience is more restricted in the case of SFE and EC. The UKES differentiates among the roles stakeholders have in the evaluation process. With respect to the functionality of the documents, the SFE Charter has a unique focus in value setting among SFE membership.

A second comparison deals with the content of the documents. Table 3.2 gives a short overview of the topics they cover.

As was true in Table 3.1, the JCS, SEVAL, and DeGEval Standards are again the most similar with respect to topics covered and in how the topics are structured and worded. This group of standards follows a cross-sectional approach; in other words, the standards are structured around topics of cross-sectional significance. For example, propriety is relevant for different actors (evaluator or commissioner) and in different phases of the evaluation process (for example, contracting, implementing, and reporting). In this respect, the JCS, SEVAL Standards, DeGEval Standards, and SFE Charter are most similar. The EC standards are structured according to the different tasks of the evaluation process. By comparison, the UKES Guidelines are oriented toward the parties involved, organized around the different roles in evaluation.

Since the EC and UKES documents use a clear-cut organizing principle (process or roles), they may be easier to communicate and apply in practice. As roles can vary heavily from evaluation to evaluation and from context to context, however, the role orientation does not allow special arrangements between the parties involved, although these special arrangements may be most appropriate in a specific case. The same holds true for the process orientation, since it restricts the flexibility to design the evaluation process in accordance with the situation at hand in a specific case.

Based on his extensive experience with the Joint Committee, Stufflebeam writes that "the participatory process leading to standards is essential" (Stufflebeam, 2003, p. 301; Stufflebeam, 2004). The distinct set of standards, including guidelines and charters, resulting from the participatory processes within the respective evaluation communities, demonstrates that evaluation has reached a higher level of professionalism. It also demonstrates that there are cultural differences among evaluation communities. Yet the most remarkable fact is that the six documents contain similar content. A detailed comparison shows that every topic covered in one document is in some way covered in the other documents as well. Nevertheless, the documents are

Table 3.2. Content of Select Standards in Europe and the Joint Committee Standards

	SEVAL Standards	DeGEval Standards	SFE Charter	UKES Guidelines	EC Standards and Practice*	Joint Committee Standards
Topics Addressed	Utility (8)	Utility (8)	Pluralism	Guidelines for evaluators (19)	Profile, role, tasks and resources of the evaluation function (8)	Utility (7)
	Feasibility (3)	Feasibility (3)	Independence	Guidelines for commissioners (18)		Feasibility (3)
	Propriety (6)	Fairness (5)	Competence	Guidelines evaluation participants (7)	Management of evaluation activities (13)	Propriety (8)
	Accuracy (10)	Accuracy (9)	Respecting the integrity of individuals	Guidelines for self-evaluation (17)	Evaluation process (12)	Accuracy (12)
			Transparency		Quality of reports (6)	
			Responsibility			
Number of standards	27	25	6	61	39	30
Structural principle	Cross-sectional	Cross-sectional	Cross-sectional	Roles	Process	Cross-sectional
Emphasized focus	Methodology	Methodology	Ethics	Deliberation	Management	Methodology

aOnly standards are addressed in this table; the EC Good Practices are not included.

distinct in the way they emphasize the issues. While the group of documents inspired by the Joint Committee Program Evaluation Standards is oriented more toward methods, the others more heavily emphasize ethics (SFE), deliberation (UKES), or management (EC). But this point should not be overemphasized since the commonalities are much more dominant than these minor shifts in orientation. In any case, the documents are in no way inconsistent or contradictory.

Outlook

Several sponsoring bodies have already begun a revision process or are planning further development of their documents. Eventual outcomes, however, are difficult to assess at the moment. In launching a second revision of the Program Evaluation Standards, the Joint Committee recently conducted a survey to get additional information about people's experiences with the standards (see Chapter Two, this issue). The DeGEval also conducted a survey to identify possible actions to take. The SEVAL standards working group is currently discussing changes and extensions in the complementary materials, although the standards are not to be changed in the near future. The UKES has declared its guidelines are not definitive and intends a continuous evaluation.

At the European level, the European Evaluation Society (EES; see www.europeanevaluation.org) has established a working group on standards, guidelines, and ethical codes in evaluation. Within this framework, it has created a Policy on Standards, Guidelines, Codes, and Principles in Evaluation (Widmer, 2004b). This policy emphasizes the cultural diversity in Europe and follows a pluralistic approach. Developing EES standards is not the intention of EES. Rather, EES supports the activities in the standards domain by promoting exchange among the organizations already active in the field of standards.

Whether future developments in Europe will be shaped more by diversity or by convergence is hard to assess. In the near future, diversity will be dominant. Whether convergence in European evaluation standards occurs in the long run is an open question. Although the use of standards or similar documents can be observed in Europe (Widmer, 2004, forthcoming), encouraging broader use of these tools in evaluation practice will be a crucial point for their future development (Neale, Owen, and Small, 2003).

References
Barbier, J.-C. *Devising and Using Evaluation Standards: The French Paradox.* Noissy-le-Grand: Centre d'études de l'emploi, 2003.
Barbier, J.-C., and Perret, B. "Ethical Guidelines and Product Quality Standards: What For?" Paper presented at the European Evaluation Society Conference, Lausanne, Switzerland, 2000.
Beywl, W. *Zur Weiterentwicklung der Evaluationsmethodologie.* Frankfurt: Lang, 1988.

Beywl, W. "Standards for Evaluation: On the Way to Guiding Principles in German Evaluation." In C. Russon (ed.), *The Program Evaluation Standards in International Settings*. Kalamazoo: Evaluation Center, Western Michigan University, 2000.

Beywl, W., and Taut, S. "Standards: Aktuelle Strategie zur Qualitätsentwicklung in der Evaluation." *Vierteljahreshefte zur Wirtschaftsforschung*, 2000, *69*, 358–370.

Bussmann, W. "Evaluation and Grassroots Politics: The Case of Switzerland." *Knowledge and Policy*, 1995, *8*(3), 85–98.

Bussmann, W. "Democracy and Evaluation's Contribution to Negotiation, Empowerment and Information." *Evaluation*, 1996, 2(3), 307–319.

Conseil scientifique de l'évaluation. *Petite guide de l'évaluation des politiques publiques*. Paris: La documentation française, 1996.

Derlien, H.-U. "Policy Evaluation in Germany: Institutional Continuation and Sectoral Activation." In J.-E. Furubo, R. Rist, and R. Sandahl (eds.), *International Atlas of Evaluation*. New Brunswick, N.J.: Transaction, 2002.

Derlien, H.-U., and Rist, R. C. "Conclusion: Policy Evaluation in International Comparison." In J.-E. Furubo, R. Rist, and R. Sandahl (eds.), *International Atlas of Evaluation*. New Brunswick, N.J.: Transaction, 2002.

European Commission Directorate General for Budget (ed.). *Evaluating EU Activities: A Practical Guide for the Commission Services*. Brussels: European Commission, 2003.

European Commission Structural Funds (ed.). *Evaluating Socio-Economics Programmes*. Luxembourg: Office for Official Publications of the European Communities, 1999.

Evaluation Research Society Standards Committee. "Evaluation Research Society Standards for Program Evaluation." In P. H. Rossi (ed.), *Standards of Evaluation Practice*. New Directions for Program Evaluation, no. 15. San Francisco: Jossey-Bass, 1982.

Fontaine, C., and Monnier, E. "Evaluation in France." In J.-E. Furubo, R. Rist, and R. Sandahl (eds.), *International Atlas of Evaluation*. New Brunswick, N.J.: Transaction, 2002.

Gray, A., and Jenkins, B. "Policy and Program Evaluation in the United Kingdom: A Reflective State?" In J.-E. Furubo, R. Rist, and R. Sandahl (eds.), *International Atlas of Evaluation*. New Brunswick, N.J.: Transaction, 2002.

Horber-Papazian, K., and Thévoz, L. "Switzerland Moving Towards Evaluation." In R. C. Rist (ed.), *Program Evaluation and the Management of Government: Patterns and Prospects Across Eight Nations*. New Brunswick, N.J.: Transaction, 1990.

Jenkins, B., and Gray, A. "Policy Evaluation in British Government: From Idealism to Realism?" In R. C. Rist (ed.), *Program Evaluation and the Management of Government: Patterns and Prospects Across Eight Nations*. New Brunswick, N.J.: Transaction, 1990.

Joint Committee on Standards for Educational Evaluation. *Standards for Evaluation of Educational Programs, Projects, and Materials*. New York: McGraw-Hill, 1981.

Joint Committee on Standards for Educational Evaluation. *The Program Evaluation Standards*. (2nd ed.) Thousand Oaks, Calif.: Sage, 1994.

Joint Committee on Standards for Educational Evaluation (ed.). *Handbuch der Evaluationsstandards*. (2nd ed.) Opladen: Leske and Budrich, 2000.

Kistler, E., and Becker, W. "Die Leiden der Evaluation." In U. Koch and W. W. Wittmann (eds.), *Evaluationsforschung*. Berlin: Springer, 1990.

Koch, U., and Wittmann, W. W. (eds.). *Evaluationsforschung*. Berlin: Springer, 1990.

Läubli Loud, M. M. "Setting Standards and Providing Guidelines: The Means Toward What End?" *Evaluation*, 2004, *10*, 237–245.

Leeuw, F. L. "Evaluation in Europe." In R. Stockmann (ed.), *Evaluationsforschung*. (2nd ed.) Opladen: Leske and Budrich, 2004.

Müller-Kohlenberg, H., and Beywl, W. "Standards der Selbstevaluation—Begründung und aktueller Diskussionsstand." *Zeitschrift für Evaluation*, 2003, no. 1, 65–75.

Neale, J., Owen, J. M., and Small, D. "Encouraging the Use of Codes of Behavior in Evaluation Practice." *Evaluation and Program Planning*, 2003, no. 26, 29–36.

Schwab, O. "The Standards of the German Evaluation Society—and Why They Are of (No?) Use for Structural Funds Evaluations in Germany." Paper presented at the Fifth European Conference on Evaluation of the Structural Funds, "Challenges for Evaluation in an Enlarged Europe," Budapest, June 2003.

Spinatsch, M. "Evaluation in Switzerland: Moving Toward a Decentralized System." In J.-E. Furubo, R. Rist, and R. Sandahl (eds.), *International Atlas of Evaluation.* New Brunswick, N.J.: Transaction, 2002.

Stockmann, R. "Evaluation in Deutschland." In R. Stockmann (ed.), *Evaluationsforschung.* (2nd ed.) Opladen: Leske and Budrich, 2004, 13–43.

Stufflebeam, D. L. "Professional Standards and Principles for Evaluations." In T. Kellaghan and D. L. Stufflebeam (eds.), *International Handbook of Educational Evaluation.* Norwell, Mass.: Kluwer, 2003.

Stufflebeam, D. L. "A Note on the Purposes, Development, and Applicability of the Joint Committee Evaluation Standards." *American Journal of Evaluation,* 2004, *25,* 99–102.

Summa, H., and Toulemonde, J. "Evaluation in the European Union: Addressing Complexity and Ambiguity." In J.-E. Furubo, R. Rist, and R. Sandahl (eds.), *International Atlas of Evaluation.* New Brunswick, N.J.: Transaction, 2002.

Toulemonde, J. "Evaluation Culture(s) in Europe: Differences and Convergence Between National Practices." *Vierteljahreshefte zur Wirtschaftsforschung,* 2000, *69,* 350–357.

United Kingdom Evaluation Society. "Guidelines for Good Practice in Evaluation." N.d. [www.evaluation.org.uk/Pub_library/Good_Practice.htm].

Widmer, T. *Meta-Evaluation: Kriterien zur Bewertung von Evaluationen.* Bern: Haupt, 1996.

Widmer, T. "Evaluating Evaluations: Does the Swiss Practice Live Up to the 'Program Evaluation Standards'?" In C. Russon (ed.), *The Program Evaluation Standards in International Settings.* Kalamazoo: Evaluation Center, Western Michigan University, 2000.

Widmer, T. "Qualität der Evaluation—Wenn Wissenschaft zur praktischen Kunst wird." In R. Stockmann (ed.), *Evaluationsforschung.* (2nd ed.) Opladen: Leske and Budrich, 2004a.

Widmer, T. *EES Policy on Standards, Guidelines, Codes and Ethics in Evaluation.* Zürich: European Evaluation Society, 2004b.

Widmer, T. "Instruments and Procedures for Assuring Evaluation Quality: A Swiss Perspective." In R. Schwartz, J. Mayne, and J. Toulemonde (eds.), *Assuring the Quality of Evaluative Information: Prospects and Pitfalls.* New Brunswick, N.J.: Transaction, forthcoming.

Widmer, T., Landert, C., and Bachmann, N. *Evaluation Standards of SEVAL, the Swiss Evaluation Society.* Geneva/Berne: SEVAL, 2000.

Widmer, T., and Neuenschwander, P. "Embedding Evaluation in the Swiss Federal Administration: Purpose, Institutional Design, and Utilization." *Evaluation,* forthcoming.

Widmer, T., Rothmayr, C., and Serdült, U. *Kurz und gut? Qualität und Effizienz von Kurzevaluationen.* Zürich: Rüegger, 1996.

Williams, K., de Laat, B., and Stern, E. *The Use of Evaluation in the Commission Services: Final Report.* Paris: Technopolis France, 2002.

THOMAS WIDMER *is a lecturer and the head of the Research Unit, Policy Analysis and Evaluation, at the Department of Political Science, University of Zürich, Switzerland.*

4

The European Commission is offered as an example of the way that governments are implementing evaluation standards.

Data- and Literature-Based Reflections on Western European Evaluation Standards and Practices

Wolfgang Beywl, Sandra Speer

Evaluation standards can be useful not only as a framework for the design but as an assessment of particular evaluations. They can also serve as indicators for the developmental stage of evaluation practice in different areas or countries. Until recently, there has not been any large-scale and comprehensive empirical investigation of knowledge and use of evaluation standards for Europe. This chapter discusses the results of one such study that used the Joint Committee Program Evaluation Standards. The study, which we undertook on behalf of the European Center for the Development of Vocational Training, is a Europe-wide empirical study on evaluation standards within the policy field of vocational training and education (VET) that includes reflections from the standpoint of users, evaluators, and researchers in the field of evaluation (Beywl and Speer, 2003, 2004).

Evaluation Standards in the Context of Vocational Education and Training in Europe

In Europe, a high percentage of evaluations take place in the context of VET programs, partly within the framework of active labor market programs or within quality management initiatives in the highly heterogeneous VET field. Literature on VET evaluation encompasses a broad palette of perspectives. Some articles focus on model theory or evaluation methods, while others report on completed evaluations.

Another clear trend is documentation that provides guidance on conducting VET evaluations. When dividing VET into micro-, meso-, and macroperspectives, we generally assign these levels to different reference disciplines. Economics tends to dominate the macroperspective. Economists often use quasi-experimental investigation forms or advanced quantitative procedures. They also employ economic theories such as human capital theory to try to explain many mesolevel phenomena. Sociological and educational methods and theories may also apply, depending on the line of investigation. The microlevel is primarily viewed from a psychological or educational perspective. Therefore, standards that are to apply specifically to VET should comply with key scientific criteria in all reference disciplines.

The objective of the study was to determine the transferability of the Joint Committee standards and the German Evaluation Society Standards (DeGEval; Deutsche Gesellschaft für Evaluation, 2002) in the European VET context. (We began from the German DeGEval Standards and their predecessors. However, this analysis concerning VET is also relevant to other European evaluation standard sets. For an overview, see Chapter Three, this issue.) Four initial questions were considered:

1. Does the terminology of the standards match the concepts in the area of European initial and continuing vocational training?
2. Are any standards not applicable in the context of initial and continuing vocational training?
3. Do European evaluation experts understand and accept the key concepts conveyed?
4. Are there any specific national differences that should be considered in defining standards?

A multimethod approach to data collection was used in the study. First, workshops were conducted with VET experts in Germany and Austria to share information about evaluation standards and solicit their opinions. Second, evaluation experts in widely divergent European countries were sent a questionnaire. Third, a literature analysis of recent European literature on VET evaluations was completed. The literature to be assessed stemmed from European authors or reflected a European background. This approach was used to prevent the unqualified import of North American evaluation culture, which could reduce acceptance and provoke resistance among the European evaluation community.

Among VET experts, the Joint Committee standards were the best-known set of evaluation standards (Beywl and Speer, 2004). These standards have been partly reflected within the frameworks of national evaluation societies and the development of their own evaluation standards. Consultation with evaluation experts showed that the term *standard* possesses very different connotations depending on national origin, academic background, and one's role in the evaluation. Colleagues from the United Kingdom associate *standard* primarily with quantified, unconditionally binding minimum standards, as, for example, in a British Standards Institute definition. Sociologists tend in their understanding to maximum standards; psychologists, at least those who are statistically inclined, tend to minimum standards. Commissioners often prefer operationalized minimum standards, particularly if they have introduced quality management systems. Evaluators favor maximum standards because they guarantee the necessary flexibility for planning and conducting evaluations.

Perusal of the literature and subsequent categorization of text segments according to individual standards consistently showed that the standards overlap (Beywl and Speer, 2004). Therefore, notes on evaluation quality requirements could not always be clearly assigned to a single standard. Overlap also stems from the fact that some standards are directly or indirectly related. The individual standards belong to extremely different analytical levels, and not all standards are equally applicable to every evaluation project. This was also true of VET evaluations. Nevertheless, the validity of each individual Joint Committee standard could be confirmed in various VET contexts.

The literature studied contained concrete quality requirements, advice, and guidance on using evaluations that resemble the individual Joint Committee standards. The individual standards in terms of the VET evaluand and its characteristics could thus be illustrated. It is noteworthy that the utility, feasibility, and propriety standards yielded many more points of reference for VET evaluations than did those of accuracy. This can be explained by the fact that the accuracy standards repeatedly formulate universal demands on empirical investigations that count not only for evaluations. Moreover, as the following section explains, certain standards could be developed further.

A Proposal for Expanding the Existing Standards

We note two gaps within the Joint Committee Program Evaluation Standards that could be clarified in the course of developing the evaluation standards. The existing standards could be expanded within the relevant individual standards or by introducing new standards. The ideas for these proposals stem from our literature review on quality requirements for program evaluations, as well as from German experiences with evaluation standards.

Selection of the Evaluation Approach. Evaluation methodology has its roots in North America, where it is widely used and has a relatively long tradition. Theorists have developed many different evaluation approaches. Each year, anthologies and textbooks introduce new variants or entirely new approaches. By contrast, with the exception of the "goal-free model" by Vedung (1998) and "realistic evaluation" by Pawson and Tilley (1997), few evaluation approaches have been developed in Europe to date. As evidenced by the European literature, numerous evaluation approaches are presented in the outline of the pluralistic-oriented evaluation standards. They differ considerably in their epistemological basis, identification of values, focus on specific elements of the evaluated program, and other issues.

Evaluation standards usually do not favor any specific evaluation approach or group of approaches. Yet some approaches, especially if they are strictly applied, may conflict with utility standards. In practice, evaluators often use an eclectic mix of evaluation approaches. In doing so, they may meet evaluation standards even if they do not know them. The reasons for selecting a particular approach and its assumed strengths and limits, however, are seldom discussed when an evaluation contract is processed.

All well-known sets of evaluation standards fail to prescribe explicit disclosure of the selected evaluation approach. (Implicitly, standards like the Joint Committee standards, 1994, contain aspects of evaluation approach selection, especially U3, Information, Scope, and Selection; U7, Evaluation Impact; the Feasibility Standards; and P1, Service Orientation.) An evaluation standard could demand specification and justification of the approaches. These approaches were used to design an evaluation, to explain why it fits the given evaluation purposes, questions, and the evaluation context. Such a standard could clarify the interaction between commissioners and contract recipients. It would also encourage more explicit presentation of evaluation theory and expose it to critical debate. In any case, evaluators should give their reasons for selecting a particular evaluation approach or combination of several and review them when the mission is accomplished. Such a standard could be especially important to young evaluation cultures and encourage propagation of evaluation approaches as well as the discussion of their strengths and weaknesses.

Selection of Suitable Methods. Choice of method is often closely linked to selection of the evaluation approach. The Joint Commission standards mention method selection frequently. Some sources scrutinize methodological aspects. Surprisingly, the standards feature no separate standard on investigation design choice and thus method justification. Methods should encourage optimal response to the evaluation questions. Evaluation textbooks (Rossi, Freeman, and Lipsey, 1999) contain short guides to selecting various methods at different points in the evaluation and for different types of evaluands.

Method selection often involves making and justifying a decision on control groups or other suitable designs. The literature frequently insists that various levels, such as micro- and macroevaluation, must be dovetailed if the evaluation is to be meaningful. It also focuses on the problems of selecting and linking quantitative and qualitative methods. Here, we discern a gap that could be closed by expanding the existing standards or by formulating a new standard. Such a standard might read: "The choice of a certain evaluation design should be justified by the evaluation questions." This would enable evaluation to explain why qualitative methods are used to answer certain questions and quantitative methods are used to answer others, and how their respective findings are jointly interpreted.

Selection of the right methods is a vital condition for evaluation success. Many evaluation methods exist, but clearly not every evaluation method is suitable for every evaluation purpose. The optimal solution depends on the questions and the solutions sought (evaluation purpose), and there is a broad range to choose from. There are so many different approaches in use that reflect the fact that no single method can be universally applied. In addition, most evaluators usually have experience applying a limited number of methods. The methods must be selected that are best for answering the prescribed questions. There must also be good alignment between the methods and the choice of evaluation approaches.

Standards for Self-Evaluation

Self-evaluation presents another area for standards expansion. In German-speaking Europe, the concept of self-evaluation has been widely propagated in the social services and the school system. Here, self-evaluation is understood in the narrow meaning; the staff members of the program (not internal or external others) control the evaluation process. Continuing vocational training programs have started introducing this process as well. Interviewed evaluators were initially uncertain whether existing evaluation standards apply to self-evaluation (Beywl and Speer, 2004).

In Germany, a first draft of self-evaluation standards has been developed (Müller-Kohlenberg and Beywl, 2003), based on the German DeGEval Standards and their predecessors. Beside utility, feasibility, propriety, and accuracy standards, they cover a new group of standards—the so-called basic conditions for self-evaluation—that encompass the following eight aspects: (1) delegation of responsibilities, (2) practitioners of self-evaluation, (3) scope of self-evaluation, (4) agreements with the management of the respective organizations, (5) procedures for publications of self-evaluation, (6) responsibilities and competencies, (7) communication among various hierarchical layers, and (8) resources for self-evaluation.

Standards Used Within the European Commission

Beside evaluation standards from national evaluation societies, commissioning organizations may develop their own standards. In this section, two standard sets at different levels from the European Commission (EC) are introduced. The first is an officially published paper giving a framework for the work of evaluation units of the EC (2003). The second is an on-line handbook, "The Guide," developed for evaluating socioeconomic development for the Directorates General (DG) Regio, which is comparable to a federal department.

The EC is designing, implementing, and evaluating policies, programs, and projects at the European level. In many cases, as for structural funds or regional policy, it designs the evaluation, but national, regional, or local authorities are in charge of implementation. Periodic evaluations include policies that do not necessarily involve monetary spending. The extent of evaluation practices varies among the different policy areas of the DGs. Most of the evaluations are contracted out to external evaluation firms or consortia. In some policy areas, evaluation occurs on the central level, on the level of the member states, and within the individual projects as well. A current example of multilayer projects financed in the scheme of the European Structural Funds (ESF) is the EQUAL initiative. It promotes new means of combating discrimination and inequalities in connection with the labor market. Many of the projects have their own internal or external evaluations running. Evaluation standards are obviously necessary to ensure evaluations of high quality, especially within these multiplayer settings.

Williams, de Laat, and Stern (2002) took a snapshot on evaluation arrangements and practices across EC services. In 2002, around one-third of the DGs applied quality standards for the evaluation function and made quality assessments of evaluation reports on a regular basis. In these DGs, the management of evaluation was accompanied by steering groups involving not only the responsible DG but also other DGs and sometimes external participants. The DGs with a high level of evaluation institutionalization exhibited important evaluation experience, sizable and trained evaluation functions, quality control and transparent procedures, and feedback mechanisms.

Directorate General Budget Standards

The evaluation unit within the DG Budget recently consolidated its function of developing and disseminating rules and guidelines for good evaluation practice. These guidelines that are also important for the other DGs. The basic elements and the development of the commission evaluation system are described in "Focus on Results: Strengthening Evaluation of Commission Activities" (EC, 2000). The commission subsequently established a set of standards and good practices in evaluation to be applied within its services: "Evaluation Standards and Good Practice." These standards were developed in collaboration with the commission's, which consists of about thirty representatives from DGs and other central European administrations. The standards consist of four chapters containing thirty-nine standards:

1. Profile, role, tasks, and resources of the evaluation function (eight standards)
2. Management of evaluation activities (thirteen standards)
3. Evaluation process (twelve standards)
4. Quality of reports (six standards)

This standard set is relevant for all DGs and their policy fields. The standard set concentrates primarily on internal evaluation systems, stressing questions of management, commissioning, and steering of evaluations. The task, reach, and framework conditions of the internal evaluation function are described in detail. Chapter C, on evaluation process, contains recommendations that concern the organization of evaluation within the administrative body of the different departments of the European Union (EU). A steering group with defined tasks will be set up. The duties of an evaluation project manager are also described in detail. Within this section, there is only one standard comparable to one of the Joint Committee Program Evaluation Standards: it states that the "persons carrying out evaluation activities shall be free of all constraints which could jeopardize their objectiveness" (C.11). The final chapter, "Quality of Reports," consists of six standards that touch on some of the Joint Committee's accuracy topics (for example, program documentation, context analysis, defensible information sources, or justified conclusions). Most questions of accuracy are mentioned merely summarily: "The substance of the evaluation reports shall be relevant, based on rigorous analysis, and meet the quality criteria laid down in the specifications" (D.1).

Although not labeled explicitly, there is a great similarity to decision- and accountability-oriented evaluation approaches (Stufflebeam, 2001). Evaluation shall "help to anticipate decision-making requirements in the fields covered by the DG or Service" (A.6.c). Most of the standards, especially in Chapters A and B, formulate guidelines of how to implement the evaluation function within the authoritative bodies of the EU. These standards are quite similar to internal administrative regulations. They enlist tasks to be done by internal evaluation units and to be negotiated with decision makers in the EU hierarchies. An obvious strength of the DG Budget standards is the clear administrative processes and regulations, the guidelines for clarifying the role of evaluation, and the mentioning of the distinctions to other approaches such as auditing, monitoring, and control. These standards also give advice on how to organize an effective feedback process of evaluation findings primarily to stakeholders and policymakers in the EU administration.

This standard set is in no way a stand-alone set because many aspects concerning methodological quality, data protection questions, and utility aspects outside the narrow user groups of the EU administrations itself are not mentioned. Often there are cross-references to other documents or evaluation standards (for example, the Joint Committee Program Evaluation Standards, DeGEval Standards, or SEVAL Standards). The regulations are formulated softly by the use of the word *shall*. Two times the verb *must* is used—once in connection with the respect opposite the evaluator's independence (C.12) and with the clauses to be included in the case of external evaluations. However, it is not clear whether there is an intentional distinction made between "must" and "should" standards.

Finally, four special points go, at least in degree, beyond the Joint Committee standards. Standard A.6.g ("demands for systematic follow-up of evaluation") notes how evaluation recommendations have been taken into account. Standard B.12 states, "Evaluation results shall be made publicly available," and D.5 strongly supports the independence of the evaluator: "The final evaluation report shall present the results and conclusions of the evaluator and the tenor shall not be amended without his/her agreement." Standard A.6.e states, "The evaluation function shall, as a minimum, define quality standards for evaluation activities on the basis of these standards and, where appropriate, its own quality requirements, more specific and detailed or better adapted to its policy area." With this paragraph, the overarching role of the DG Budget standards is manifested. In this sense, the most encompassing and recently revised guidelines of the evaluation function are represented by the MEANS handbooks and "The Guide."

The "Golden Rules" and the MEANS Grid of "The Guide"

In 1999, the EC published the MEANS (Methods for Evaluating Structural Policies) collection. Volume Five of this collection contains a framework to assess the quality of evaluation reports that includes several standards that overlap with some of the Joint Committee Program Evaluation Standards (Beywl and Widmer, 2000). Since this first edition, there have been many changes and developments in EC evaluation practice. The political priorities concerning structural policies have been shifted to areas such as human and social capital, knowledge economy, and equal opportunities. The evaluation designs accordingly changed to different evaluation focuses, as well as newly developed evaluation approaches and methods. Moreover, the ten new member states have strong evaluation capacity-building needs.

As a follow-up to the MEANS collection, a comprehensive guide for evaluations of socioeconomic development programs was published on the Internet in 2003 (EC, 1999). The intended readers of "The Guide" (EC, 2003) belong to different groups such as policymakers, commissioners of evaluation, program managers, program partners, and, of course, evaluators. For evaluators, "The Guide" provides not only evaluation theory and philosophy, but also many resources, such as data collection methods on a how-to level. Each of the four chapters is accompanied by "golden rules." These golden rules consist of good practices as well as rules of thumb, and they represent a set of reference points comparable to evaluation standards.

The ten golden rules concerning the "contribution of evaluation to socio-economic development" focus partly on utility aspects as they can be found within the respective group of the Joint Committee standards (stakeholder identification or report timeliness). They stress the "service orientation" (Joint Committee, 1994, P1) very strongly by engaging the evaluation especially to the needs of "the intended beneficiaries of the program interventions" (1.9).

The next ten golden rules, on designing and implementing evaluation, relate to evaluability assessment, stakeholder involvement, evaluation commissioning and management, evaluation questions, and process and output use, as well as respective quality assurance. These rules also touch main issues from the Joint Commission utility and feasibility standards. They point to snares such as the restriction of the examination to explicit goals (for example, neglecting unintended effects) or lacking responsiveness with respect to the interests of the information needs of stakeholders.

The eleven golden rules on evaluation capacity building are really an addition to the scope of the Joint Committee Standards. (The only evaluation standards of a national evaluation society that examine organizational learning are the French standards.) Evaluation capacity building is seen as an essential prerequisite for the commissioning, steering, and use of evaluations. Capacity building is understood not solely as a top-down process, but also as strengthening cooperative links and the demand side.

Part Four of "The Guide," on "choosing methods, techniques and indicators and using evidence in evaluation," incorporates thirteen golden rules. They are tailored to socioeconomic evaluations and concentrate on utility aspects, qualitative methods and data quality, and indicator systems, as well as choosing evaluators and evaluation teams. It is not clear why only qualitative methods are privileged. Some of the golden rules take a strong position against ill-implemented approaches of monitoring systems or performance management, such as "over elaborated indicator systems."

As mentioned in several rules, the scope of "The Guide" is restricted to evaluations of socioeconomic development programs. Certainly there is potential to transfer many parts of this resource to other evaluation fields such as health. Another restriction, however, is more implicit. There are several arguments that state that evaluation should be focused on, if not restricted to, formative evaluation: "Evaluations must be fully integrated into program planning and management" (P1.4). It is not absolutely clear how to deal with the summative evaluation function or whether it is seen as represented by other approaches such as performance management. "The Guide" seems to favor value-prioritizing evaluation approaches that provide widely accepted values as a basis for the evaluation and its results (for a classification of evaluation models, see Beywl, Speer, and Kehr, 2004).

Within "The Guide," two MEANS grids are reproduced: one concerns quality control (output criteria) and the other quality assurance (process criteria). These MEANS grids are at different levels of ensuring evaluative quality than the golden rules. The latter refer more to the quality of evaluation systems in the context of the structural funds, while the former refer to the specific judgments in evaluation reports and outputs in this area. The MEANS grid was established for assessing evaluation reports by the evaluation units and by the steering groups (EC, 1999). As the output criteria are used for intermediary reports, they can acquire the character of minimum standards, although unforeseen circumstances are considered. Meanwhile, they have also been used for metaevaluations on a national level (Uusikylä and Virtanen, 2000). In the MEANS handbooks from 1999, output criteria were rated on four-mark scales, with two marks being negative and two being positive. In the new grid (EC, 2003), an intermediary neutral score has been added. The judgments made on the basis of the grids may require improvements or even the rejection of interim or final evaluation reports.

Outlook

Until now, the development of evaluation standards has taken place largely independently in the regions of the world. A look at European politics in the light of the Joint Committee Program Evaluation Standards shows that there are still dialogue deficits but also great opportunities. The standards of neither the DG Budget nor "The Guide" contain an explicit discussion of the content of the Joint Committee standards, although references show that the authors clearly know the Joint Committee standards. Developers could have perhaps avoided some shortcomings of these new and promising rule sets by taking the Joint Committee standards more seriously into account. Perhaps it is not an easy exercise for a young, still-forming European evaluation community, in itself international and intercultural, to align to the U.S. standards tradition without risking its identity. Nevertheless, evaluation worldwide is in a strong competitive situation with other approaches, such as auditing or quality management, that have reached a much stronger disciplinary identity than evaluation, on the European level (Beywl and Widmer, 2000) and internationally. For example, the European Foundation for Quality Management (EFQM) has more than 700 member organizations based in more than 50 countries worldwide. Its EFQM Excellence Model is not only used as the criterion for the awarding process, but it serves as a management tool, including a broad scope of self-assessment tools. In Europe, about 20,000 organizations are working with this model, and a growing number of nonprofit or social service organizations are also using the model (http://www.efqm.org). As an international example, the International Standards for the Professional Practice of Internal Auditing are developed and disseminated by the Institute of Internal Auditors' 93,000 members worldwide in 160 countries, having chapters or institutes in more than 90 countries (http://www.theiia.org/ iia/index.cfm). Evaluation is competing with these other disciplines for market share. The worldviews of society and the individual that underpin the various disciplines are also competing.

The Joint Committee standards are clear and complete with respect to evaluation as a systematic process to describe and assess the value of programs based on empirical inquiry. However, the standards of the European Commission emphasize framework conditions that must be created and assured for internal evaluations. The golden rules from "The Guide" are helpful, especially as they pertain to evaluation capacity building. These differences concerning strengths and weaknesses of these different standard sets can be used productively if the international exchange on evaluation standards can be strengthened.

References

Beywl, W., and Speer, S. "Qualitätskriterien für Evaluationen in der Berufsbildung." *Berufsbildung in Wissenschaft und Praxis*, 2003, no. 6, 13–17.

Beywl, W., and Speer, S. "Developing Standards to Evaluate Vocational Education and Training Programs." In P. Descy and M. Tessaring (eds.), *The Foundations of Evaluation and Impact Research: Third Report on Vocational Training Research in Europe—Background Report*. Luxembourg: Office for Official Publications of the European Communities, 2004.

Beywl, W., Speer, S., and Kehr, J. *Wirkungsorientierte Evaluation im Rahmen der Armut-sund Reichtumsberichterstattung*. Bonn: Bundesministerium für Gesundheit und Soziale Sicherung, 2004.

Beywl, W., and Widmer, T. "Die Standards im Vergleich mit weiteren Regelwerken zur Qualität fachlicher Leistungserstellung." In J. R. Sanders (eds.), *Joint Committee on Standards for Educational Evaluation*. Opladen: Leske & Budrich, 2000.

Deutsche Gesellschaft für Evaluation (ed.). *Standards für Evaluation*. Cologne: Deutsche Gesellschaft für Evaluation, 2002.

European Commission. *The MEANS Collection, European Communities*. Luxembourg: European Commission, 1999.

European Commission. "Focus on Results: Strengthening Evaluation of Commission Activities," Brussels, 2000. [http://europa. eu.int/comm/budget/evaluation/pdf/sec20001051_en.pdf].

European Commission. "Evaluation Standards and Good Practice: Brussels, 2002." [http://europa.eu.int/comm/budget/evaluation/pdf/C_ 2002_5267_final_en.pdf].

European Commission. "Evaluation of Socio-Economic Development—The Guide." 2003. [www.evalsed.info/frame_guide_intro.asp].

Joint Committee on Standards for Educational Evaluation. *The Program Evaluation Standards*. (2nd ed.) Thousand Oaks, Calif.: Sage, 1994.

Joint Committee on Standards for Educational Evaluation. *Handbuch der Evaluationsstandards*. Opladen: Leske & Budrich, 2000.

Müller-Kohlenberg, H., and Beywl, W. "Standards der Selbstevaluation." *Zeitschrift für Evaluation*, 2003, no. 3, 79–93.

Pawson, J. M., and Tilley, N. *Realistic Evaluation*. Thousand Oaks, Calif.: Sage, 1997.

Rossi, P. H., Freeman, H. E., and Lipsey, M. W. *Evaluation: A Systematic Approach*. Thousand Oaks, Calif.: Sage, 1999.

Stufflebeam, D. L. (ed.). *Evaluation Models*. New Directions for Evaluation, no. 89. San Francisco: Jossey-Bass, 2001.

Uusikylä, P., and Virtanen, P. "Meta-Evaluation as a Tool for Learning: A Case Study of the European Structural Fund Evaluations in Finland." *Evaluation*, 2000, 6(1), 50–65.

Vedung, E. *Evaluation im öffentlichen Sektor*. Vienna: Boehlau, 1998.

Williams, K., de Laat, B., and Stern, E. *The Use of Evaluation in the Commission Services: Final Report*. Paris: Technopolis France, 2002.

WOLFGANG BEYWL is founder of Univation Institute for Evaluation in Cologne, Germany, and director of the postgraduate studies program in evaluation at Berne University, Switzerland.

SANDRA SPEER is associate at Univation Institute for Evaluation in Cologne, Germany.

5

A description of the complex geographical and cultural context of the African Evaluation Guidelines, with special emphasis on the role of the African Evaluation Association, is followed by a discussion of the development of the guidelines, their implementation, and use.

The Origin and Development of the African Evaluation Guidelines

Jean-Charles Rouge

Africa is a vast continent of some 11.7 million square miles (30.3 million square kilometers). It is divided into fifty-three independent nations and ranks second only to Asia in size. The African continent represents about 20 percent of the earth's total landmass, yet its population represents only around 10 percent of the world's total population, ranking third in the world, behind Asia and Europe, in continental population (Crandall, 2003).

Most of the African landmass is high in elevation, although it has relatively few mountain ranges. The highest point is Mount Kilimanjaro, at an elevation of 19,340 feet (5,895 meters) above the East African plains in Tanzania. The Nile, the longest river in the world, flows more than 4,000 miles (6,400 kilometers) from its origin at Lake Victoria to the Mediterranean Sea. Other major rivers on the continent are the Congo, the Niger, and the Zambezi. There are many islands off the coast of Africa, including Madagascar, the fourth largest island in the world (229,000 square miles, or 593,000 square kilometers). Because it straddles the equator, Africa has warm temperatures most of the year. However, the temperatures are moderated somewhat in high elevations and by ocean currents along the coast (Crandall, 2003).

Africa is divided geographically and culturally into two separate regions. The Sahara Desert, comparable in size to the United States, dominates the landscape of northern Africa. Historically and culturally, North Africa is predominantly Mediterranean, Arabic, and Muslim. South of the Sahara is Black Africa. This part of the continent hosts an incredible diversity of peoples and cultures, and more than one thousand languages and dialects are spoken. Economies vary from mostly developed (South Africa) to agricultural to hunting and gathering (Crandall, 2003).

European colonial powers drew the current political boundaries of African countries in the mid- to late nineteenth century. Thus, many peoples who shared a similar culture found themselves divided into two or three different geographical sections, each belonging to a different colony. Independence from Europe began in the 1960s and finally ended with Namibian independence in 1991. African nations have had to struggle with a colonial legacy as well as increasing populations, heavy urbanization, low economic growth, civil war, ethnic violence, educational franchise, limited health care delivery, and disease. They have met these challenges with varying degrees of success and failure. The continent as a whole is rich in natural and human resources with great social and economic potential, yet the future of Africa is difficult to predict (Crandall, 2003).

Development of Program Evaluation in Africa

In May 1990, the first evaluation seminar in Africa took place in Côte d'Ivoire (African Development Bank and World Bank, 1998). It was the first in a series of regional seminars on evaluation planned by the Development Assistance Committee (DAC) of the Organization for Economic Cooperation and Development (OECD). The seminar was jointly presented by the DAC and African Development Bank (ADB). Objectives of this first meeting included the clarification of evaluation needs as perceived by African countries and an exploration of ways to strengthen self-evaluation capacities. It would be another eight years before a second major evaluation seminar to address the clarified needs took place on the continent.

During the interim, many grassroots activities took place, one of the most successful of which was the Nairobi Monitoring and Evaluation Network in Kenya. Mahesh Patel, the regional evaluation officer for UNICEF's Eastern and Southern Africa Regional Office, convened the network. Evaluators in Nairobi would meet together once a month at the U.N. compound and make informal presentations to build each other's capacity. Although an informal evaluation organization, the Nairobi Monitoring and Evaluation Network was represented on the President's Panel at the 1998 American Evaluation Association conference (Russon and Love, 1999).

November 1998 saw the first of five major evaluation conferences to take place during the following seven years. The conference, sponsored by the ADB and the World Bank (1998), was again held in Côte d'Ivoire, the site of the evaluation seminar that had taken place eight years earlier. The event brought participants from many parts of Africa together with a large number of representatives from development assistance agencies. The agenda consisted of plenary presentations on general themes and parallel sessions that were held around the themes of resources, partnerships, participation, and feedback as they pertained to building evaluation supply and demand.

In the final two days, workshops were organized to help participants develop their own evaluation capacity development plans.

The following year, under the guidance of Mahesh Patel and Kate Spring, the evaluation organizations in Comoros, Kenya, Madagascar, Malawi, Niger, and Rwanda organized a major conference in Kenya, at which the African Evaluation Association (AfrEA) was inaugurated. Over 350 evaluators and development practitioners from 35 countries attended the conference. There were seven parallel strands in which eighty-eight papers on evaluation in Africa were presented. Michael Quinn Patton, author of *Utilization-Focused Evaluation* (1997), provided keynote training sessions. Work groups developed plans of action including adaptation of the North American evaluation standards for Africa, formation of national evaluation organizations, and ratification of the "The AfrEA Declaration" to formally launch the AfrEA (C. Russon, personal communication to M. Scriven, 1999).

In September 2000, delegates from the national evaluation organizations in Kenya, Niger, and Rwanda participated in the World Bank's Regional Workshop and Seminar on Monitoring and Evaluation Capacity Development for Africa held in South Africa (Development Bank of Southern Africa, African Development Bank, and World Bank, 2000). These delegates were joined by others representing African national governments, nongovernmental organizations, universities, research institutes, the private sector, and multilateral and bilateral donor agencies. At this meeting, preliminary thoughts on the International Development Evaluation Association (IDEAS) were introduced by the U.N. Development Programme and the World Bank. IDEAS is a voluntary association devoted to the advancement of development evaluation.

The Second AfrEA Conference, held in Kenya in 2002, brought together evaluators, researchers, policymakers, evaluation users, and donors from Africa, Europe, Asia, New Zealand, Colombia, and the United States. Discussions and presentations on major development issues in Africa were held in twelve topical strands. Recommendations aimed at taking AfrEA into the next phase of development were accepted; subsequent to the conference, national leaders and donors made several decisions about the future of AfrEA. An executive committee was constituted and key priorities identified. It was also decided that a third AfrEA conference would take place in South Africa within two years.

The third conference is being planned for December 2004 on the theme "Africa Matters, Evaluation Matters: Joining Forces for Democracy, Governance, and Development." The conference will consist of a wide variety of parallel strands, preceded by evaluation capacity-building workshops. Several organizations, such as International Organization for Cooperation in Evaluation (IOCE), IDEAS, and the DAC/OECD Network on Development Evaluation, will host special sessions. Well-known international and African evaluation specialists will give presentations. There will be opportunities for debate and networking between stakeholder groups, and strategies will be mapped to improve the theory and practice of evaluation in Africa.

In summary, eight years transpired between the first major evaluation seminar and the second. In the 1990s, African evaluators began forming their own regional and national evaluation organizations. These evaluation organizations appear to have been able to engage bilateral and multilateral donor agencies as partners in the effort to develop evaluation capacity on the continent.

Development of African Evaluation Guidelines

During a 1998 UNICEF regional workshop in Nairobi, "UNICEF ESARO Technical Training Workshop in Evaluation Methodology," a North American program evaluation standards training session and a focus group demonstration were conducted (Russon, 1998). During the demonstration, the participants were asked to discuss the appropriateness of the North American evaluation standards for use in African cultures, including the appropriateness of the four categories of standards. The following year, Patel and Russon produced a paper that detailed the modifications deemed necessary by the participants in order for the North American standards to be useful in an African setting. The paper was discussed at various forums, including meetings of the Nairobi Monitoring and Evaluation Network, at a plenary session at the Inaugural Conference of the African Evaluation Association (Patel and Russon, 1999), and at a Southern African Development Bank regional workshop (Patel and Russon, 2000).

The Patel and Russon paper served to guide the development of what has come to be called the African Evaluation Guidelines (AEG; see the chapter appendix). The guidelines remain loosely based on the Program Evaluation Standards (Joint Committee on Standards for Educational Evaluation, 1994). The main modifications focused on the changes necessitated by the political and cultural differences between Africa and the United States as well as other developed countries. For example, an important issue for the guidelines concerned with political and governance issues was the need to protect evaluators from authoritarian governments. The consensus text provides more protection than would be needed by evaluators working in more liberal settings. Other significant changes due to differences in political settings include the guidelines on political viability and disclosure of findings.

After an extended period of review and discussion, eleven networks and associations of evaluators in Africa presented a consolidated version of the AEG at the second AfrEA conference with the following recommendations:

- National networks and evaluation associations should adopt the AEG as their core standards and use them to develop terms of reference, report validation through metaevaluation, and dissemination phases.

- Governments and public bodies should encourage the use of the guidelines to ensure harmony, consistency, accountability, quality, and ownership of evaluation.
- U.N. agencies and other multinational organizations should take up the challenge of using the guidelines as corporate standards in evaluation.

Before the recommendations were adopted, an exchange took place between organizers of the conference and the gender strand representatives. (As already noted, the second AfrEA conference was organized around twelve topical strands, one of which dealt with gender issues.) The strand representatives maintained that the AEG should reflect their gender modifications and insights. They proposed various modalities to achieve this, such as the inclusion of an appendix, posting the outcomes of the discussion on the Web site, or adding a preamble to the guideline on gender equality as an underlying core principle. In the end, consensus was reached to revisit the exact modality to be used and to let the gender strand representatives take up the task of auditing the guidelines. This compromise opened the way for the eventual adoption of the guidelines.

The AEG is a living document. AfrEA will work with national evaluation associations in Africa on further development as well as implementation. As the guidelines have been translated into various languages and are accessible to more people across the continent, additional insights and lessons are likely to lead to new modifications. The AEG will also be enriched by the insights from OECD's Development Assistance Committee's criteria and other related work. Forums created through organizations such as the International Organization for Cooperation in Evaluation (IOCE) and the International Development Evaluation Association (IDEAS) will help shape further conceptual thought on their development and application.

Implementation and Use of Standards

African countries are in the early stages of implementation of the AEG. Significant effort has been invested in the elaboration of the guidelines and their promotion in key international evaluation conferences. Nevertheless, it takes time in any environment to disseminate, institutionalize, and endorse standards in the midst of the international development community and their national counterparts, such as governments, civil society organizations, universities, and consulting firms at the country level. Africa is no exception in this process.

Since 1999, UNICEF has undertaken a series of tests mostly in Eastern and Southern African countries, including a country program evaluation in Central African Republic, a midterm review in Eritrea, and a meta-evaluation of fourteen UNICEF/UNAIDS HIV/AIDS programs' evaluations throughout Eastern and Southern Africa. One measure of success in taking the AEG into a more accepted venue is the fact that UNICEF has added some components of the AEG on its own and a global set of program evaluation standards to better fit the African context.

As long as UNICEF local monitoring and evaluation officers are not required to systematically use the AEG in their evaluation work, knowledge and lessons of effectiveness must be drawn from a more limited pool of evaluations that use AEG in the field. Currently, there appears to be an imbalance in field testing among Eastern, Southern, Western, and Central Africa. Eastern and Southern Africa have more experience than Western and Central Africa, where only one case has been registered in Central African Republic. Under such circumstances, neither real implementation nor institutionalization of the AEG has been observed. It is also worth noting that most of international multidonor, bilateral organizations, and international nongovernmental organizations have developed their own program evaluation standards. Performance monitoring systems are based primarily on either the Program Evaluation Standards (Joint Committee on Standards for Educational Evaluation, 1994) or the OECD/DAC criteria. Under such a position, the AEG are considered by these organizations as an additional source of inspiration to eventually improve their own quality assessment checklists rather than as a tool to replace existing ones.

The U.N. Evaluation Group is working to establish a set of common evaluation norms and standards that will replace the current U.N. rules and regulations on evaluation. It aims to improve the quality of evaluation based on their more active use. A meeting led by UNICEF in Geneva in 2004 made considerable progress on the norms and standards. There is no direct use or endorsement of the AEG within the organization; however, references have been made to the U.S. Program Evaluation Standards on which the AEG are based. In fact, if one broadens the standards to incorporate these other sets, it becomes difficult to know who is using what.

The implementation and use of the AEG at a larger scale in Africa is a real challenge. At the country level, governments, civil society organizations, universities, research centers, and consulting firms could benefit the most from effective implementation and use of the AEG in their respective monitoring and evaluation practices. A common view on that issue asserts that to guarantee greater ownership of development programs and projects and better-managed development, the implementation and institutionalization of the AEG aim to provide national evaluator communities with a tool to engage in a lasting learning process. This would improve governments' decision-making skills based on high-quality evaluations.

It is worth noting that decisions involving significant expenditures, people's lives, or the future of an organization may rely on the results of a program evaluation. Evaluation capacity development in Africa has been an ongoing process and a critical issue for a decade. Nearly all African countries have poor national statistics information systems, low-skilled human resources, unsatisfactory political awareness, unwillingness to allocate more funds to evaluation, and low capacities among public administrations.

Furthermore, many African nations are young democracies lacking a comprehensive participatory and evaluation culture. Under such circumstances, neither evaluation standards nor the AEG can easily be implemented or used by government bodies and the other categories of local actors despite what is at stake. Further analysis may well be warranted.

National and regional monitoring and evaluation networks and associations have a key role to play in promoting the use of program evaluation standards in general and of the AEG in particular. A major constraint for the implementation of the AEG is that informal national monitoring and evaluation networks have elaborated this document, raising delicate credibility and representative issues for international and national partners. Endorsement and advocacy coordinated at the level of the New Partnership for Africa's Development Secretariat (www.nepad.org) or the African Union could have a significant impact on the spread and institutionalization of the AEG in the continent.

Parallel to this set of core constraints, one must bear in mind that recent movements in development practices in Africa and, hence, in development evaluation, have stressed the importance of having such standards and guidelines more than ever before. The welcome shift to country-led development has accelerated the need for country-led evaluation. Country-led development can be defined by country ownership, not just government ownership, of development, and country-led development partnerships, which starts to shift traditional asymmetrical relationships with donors. This approach will support trends such as a more holistic approach to development, a longer-term view of development, and a results-based approach to development. For example, there is now a need for greater local evaluation capacity, more accountability, and results-based work. Therefore, the demands on evaluation, the impact evaluation has, and its potential audience will probably be greater in Africa than ever before. Because of these, there is a need for greater emphasis on quality and ethics. Clearly, evaluations must consider much more complex frameworks and environments, which require conceptually strong-skilled evaluators.

New tools are necessary for sustainable evaluation capacities in Africa. National and regional monitoring, evaluation networks, and associations must be strengthened and linked with academic centers to form think-tanks, knowledge, and advocacy networks. Monitoring and evaluation training must be intensified and adapted to meet new challenges. Civil society must be nurtured by an understanding of and demand for monitoring and evaluation. Local evaluation communities must engage in concerted in-depth development evaluation research on critical issues for appropriate, innovative monitoring and evaluation theory and practice. Therefore, there is an important need to respect, take note of, and mobilize indigenous evaluation knowledge that should drive research. Publication by local evaluators is an important component to developing capacity.

Conclusion

This contextualization of the use of the AEG gives a picture of the complexity in implementing AEG in Africa. There is a great need for evaluators in all geographies, particularly those from developed countries working in Africa, to understand local contexts and incorporate guidelines and standards, when available, that understand local context and respect the local people and their culture.

Appendix: The African Evaluation Guidelines: 2002

A checklist to assist in planning evaluations, negotiating clear contracts, reviewing progress and ensuring adequate completion of an evaluation.

Nairobi MandE Network, African Evaluation Association Secretariat, Réseau Nigérien de Suivi et Evaluation, Cape Verde Evaluation Network, Réseau Malagache de Suivi et Evaluation, Comoros Evaluation Network, Eritrean Evaluation Network, Malawi MandE Network, Réseau National de Chercheurs et Evaluateurs de Burundi, Rwanda Evaluation Network, UNICEF Eastern and Southern Africa Region MandE Network

• Utility: The utility guidelines are intended to ensure that an evaluation will serve the information needs of intended users *and be owned by stakeholders.*

U1 (modified) *Stakeholder Identification.* Persons *and organizations* involved in or affected by the evaluation (with special attention to beneficiaries at community level) should be identified *and included in the evaluation process,* so that their needs can be addressed *and so that the evaluation findings are utilizable and owned by stakeholders, to the extent this is useful, feasible and allowed.*

U2 *Evaluator Credibility.* The persons conducting the evaluation should be both trustworthy and competent to perform the evaluation, so that the evaluation findings achieve maximum credibility and acceptance.

U3 *Information Scope and Selection.* Information collected should be broadly selected to address pertinent questions about the program and be responsive to the needs and interests of clients and other specified stakeholders.

U4 (modified) *Values Identification.* The perspectives, procedures, and rationale used to interpret the findings should be carefully described, so that the bases for value judgments are clear. *The possibility of allowing multiple interpretations of findings should be transparently preserved, provided that these interpretations respond to stakeholders' concerns and needs for utilization purposes.*

U5 *Report Clarity.* Evaluation reports should clearly describe the program being evaluated, including its context, and the purposes, procedures, and findings of the evaluation, so that essential information is provided and easily understood.

U6 (*modified*) *Report Timeliness and Dissemination.* Significant interim find-ings and evaluation reports should be disseminated to intended users, so that they can be used in a reasonably timely fashion, *to the extent that this is useful, feasible and allowed. Comments and feedback of intended users on interim findings should be taken into consideration prior to the production of the final report.*

U7 *Evaluation Impact.* Evaluations should be planned, conducted, and reported in ways that encourage follow through by stakeholders, so that the likelihood that the evaluation will be used is increased.

- Feasibility: The feasibility guidelines are intended to ensure that an evaluation will be realistic, prudent, diplomatic, and frugal.

F1 *Practical Procedures.* The evaluation procedures should be practical, to keep disruption to a minimum while needed information is obtained.

F2 (*modified*) *Political Viability.* The evaluation should be planned and con-ducted with anticipation of the different positions of various interest groups, so that their cooperation may be obtained, and so that possible attempts by any of these groups to curtail evaluation operations or to bias or misapply the results can be averted or counteracted *to the extent that this is feasible in the given institutional and national situation.*

F3 (*modified*) *Cost Effectiveness.* The evaluation should be efficient and produce information of sufficient value, so that the resources expended can be justified. *It should keep within its budget and account for its own expenditures.*

- Propriety—The propriety guidelines are intended to ensure that an evaluation will be conducted legally, ethically, and with due regard for the welfare of those involved in the evaluation, as well as those affected by its results.

P1 *Service Orientation.* Evaluation should be designed to assist organizations to address and effectively serve the needs of the full range of targeted par-ticipants.

P2 (*modified*) *Formal Agreements.* Obligations of the formal parties to an evaluation (what is to be done, how, by whom, when) should be agreed to *through dialogue and in writing, to the extent that this is feasible and appropriate, so that these parties have a common understanding of all the con-ditions of the agreement and hence are in a position to* formally renegotiate it if necessary. *Specific attention should be paid to informal and implicit aspects of expectations of all parties to the contract.*

P3 (*modified*) *Rights of Human Participants.* Evaluation should be designed and conducted to respect and protect the rights and welfare of human subjects *and the communities of which they are members. The confidential-ity of personal information collected from various sources must be strictly protected.*

P4 (modified) Human Interaction. Evaluators should respect human dignity and worth in their interactions with other persons associated with an evaluation, so that participants are not threatened or harmed *or their cultural or religious values compromised.*

P5 Complete and Fair Assessment. The evaluation should be complete and fair in its examination and recording of strengths and weaknesses of the program being evaluated, so that strengths can be built upon and problem areas addressed.

P6 (modified) Disclosure of Findings. The formal parties to an evaluation should ensure that the full set of evaluation findings along with pertinent limitations are made accessible to the persons affected by the evaluation, and any others with expressed legal rights to receive the results *as far as possible. The evaluation team and the evaluating institution will determine what is deemed possible, to ensure that the needs for confidentiality of national or governmental entities and of the contracting agents are respected, and that the evaluators are not exposed to potential harm.*

P7 Conflict of Interest. Conflict of interest should be dealt with openly and honestly, so that it does not compromise the evaluation processes and results.

P8 Fiscal Responsibility. The evaluator's allocation and expenditure of resources should reflect sound accountability procedures and otherwise be prudent and ethically responsible, so that expenditures are accounted for and appropriate.

- Accuracy—The accuracy guidelines are intended to ensure that an evaluation will reveal and convey technically adequate information about the features that determine worth of merit of the program being evaluated.

A1 (modified) Program Documentation. The program being evaluated should be described clearly and accurately, so that the program is clearly identified, *with attention paid to personal and verbal communications as well as written records.*

A2 (modified) Context Analysis. The context in which the program exists should be examined in enough detail, including *political, social, cultural and environmental aspects,* so that its likely influences on the program can be identified and assessed.

A3 Described Purposes and Procedures. The purposes and procedures of the evaluation should be monitored and described in enough detail, so that they can be identified and assessed.

A4 (modified) Defensible Information Sources. The sources of information used in a program evaluation should be described in enough detail, so that the adequacy of the information can be assessed, *without compromising any necessary anonymity or cultural or individual sensitivities of respondents.*

A5 (modified) Valid Information. The information gathering procedures should be chosen or developed and then implemented so that they will assure that the implementation arrived at is valid for the intended use. *Information that is likely to be susceptible to biased reporting should be checked using a range of methods and from a variety of sources.*

A6 Reliable Information. The information gathering procedures should be chosen or developed and then implemented so that they will assure that the information obtained is sufficiently reliable for the intended use.

A7 Systematic Information. The information collected, processed, and reported in an evaluation should be systematically reviewed and any errors found should be corrected.

A8 Analysis of Quantitative Information. Quantitative information in an evaluation should be appropriately and systematically analyzed so that evaluation questions are effectively answered.

A9 Analysis of Qualitative Information. Qualitative information in an evaluation should be appropriately and systematically analyzed so that evaluation questions are effectively answered.

A10 Justified Conclusions. The conclusions reached in an evaluation should be explicitly justified, so that stakeholders can assess them.

A11 Impartial Reporting. Reporting procedures should guard against distortion caused by personal feelings and biases of any party to the evaluation, so that evaluation reports fairly reflect the evaluation findings.

A12 Meta-Evaluation. The evaluation itself should be formatively and summatively evaluated against these and other pertinent guidelines, so that its conduct is appropriately guided and, on completion, stakeholders can closely examine its strengths and weakness.

Source: Nairobi M&E Network and others (2002).

References

African Development Bank and the World Bank, Operations Evaluation Department. *Evaluation Capacity Development in Africa: Selected Proceedings from a Seminar and in Abidjan.* Washington, D.C.: African Development Bank and the World Bank, 1998.

Crandall, D. *Africa.* Lindon, Utah: Axiom Press, 2003.

Development Bank of Southern Africa, African Development Bank, and World Bank. *Monitoring and Evaluation Capacity Development in Africa: Selected Proceedings from a Seminar and Workshop.* Washington, D.C.: Development Bank of Southern Africa, African Development Bank, and World Bank, 2000.

Joint Committee on Standards for Educational Evaluation. *The Program Evaluation Standards.* Thousand Oaks, Calif.: Sage, 1994.

Nairobi M&E Network and others. *The African Evaluation Guidelines.* Nairobi, Kenya: AfrEA, 2002.

Patel, M., and Russon, C. "Appropriateness of the Program Evaluation Standards for Use in African Cultures." Paper presented at the inaugural meeting of the African Evaluation Association, Nairobi, Kenya, 1999.

Patel, M., and Russon, C. "Appropriateness of the Program Evaluation Standards for Use in African Cultures." *Monitoring and Evaluation Capacity Development in Africa: Selected Proceedings from a Seminar and Workshop.* Johannesburg, South Africa: Development Bank of Southern Africa, African Development Bank, and World Bank, 2000.

Patton, M. Q. *Utilization-Focused Evaluation: The New Century Text.* (3rd ed.) Thousand Oaks, Calif.: Sage, 1997.

Russon, C. UNICEF ESARO Technical Training Workshop in Evaluation Methodology, Nairobi, Kenya, Oct. 5–9, 1998.

Russon, C., and Love, A. (eds.). "Creating a World-Wide Evaluation Community." Kalamazoo: Evaluation Center, Western Michigan University, 1999.

JEAN-CHARLES ROUGE is a monitoring and evaluation specialist with the U.N. Development Program, a coordinator of the NIGER Monitoring and Evaluation Network, and an executive board member of the African Evaluation Association.

*The author discusses the history and current status of the
Australasian Evaluation Society's standards-setting
activities.*

National Evaluation Standards for Australia and New Zealand: Many Questions but Few Answers

Doug Fraser

Australia and New Zealand stand out as something of an anomaly in the
international trend toward developing common standards for evaluation.
The national professional association that covers evaluation in both countries, the Australasian Evaluation Society (AES), was one of the earliest and
most proactive in developing a comprehensive code of practitioner ethics.
However, despite having the issue on its agenda since the late 1980s, some
feel there is a lack of resolution on quality standards (Fraser, 2001a, 2001b).

In planning this chapter, I formed a small reference group that
included half a dozen prominent members of the AES with a history of
involvement in ethical and standards issues. Their backgrounds included
government, higher education, and private consulting, with experience
dating back in some cases to the 1970s. In the course of our discussions,
even where they related solely to Australia, it was often hard to believe
that we were talking about the same country. Reaching a set of agreed gen-
eralizations about the status, the context, and history of evaluation proved

I wish to acknowledge the advice and contributions of Ian Trotman and Jerome Winston
in helping me to sort out a complicated story that stretches back into the mists of a time
well before mine. Without their invaluable corporate memory, it would have been
impossible to write this chapter. Other Australasian Evaluation Society members who
have kept an eye on the progress of this chapter are Colin Sharp, David Turner (current
chair of the ethics and standards committee), Chris Milne, and Nan Wehipeihana. The
opinions expressed, though thoroughly discussed with other members of the group, are
ultimately my own.

extraordinarily difficult. Given the diversity of opinions, it is impossible to give a balanced account of the evaluation practice in both countries. Readers are cautioned to treat this chapter as a snapshot of one person's experience and point of view, reflected in the opinion-based comments provided here. Historical information in this chapter is drawn primarily from Sharp, 2003; Trotman, 2003; Lunt and Trotman, forthcoming; and Ryan, 2003. It is supplemented by personal communications from Ian Trotman and Jerome Winston.

Geographical Context

Australia and New Zealand, sometimes grouped together under the common title "Australasia," were the two most important centers of British colonization in the Indian and Pacific Ocean region, and today they are the only significant countries in the Southern Hemisphere, outside South America, where the dominant culture derives from Europe. They are independent countries within the British Commonwealth, separated by some sixteen hundred kilometers of sea, but they have a number of common institutions, especially in professional fields.

Geographical distance, together with relatively small populations for the land area, have shaped the consciousness and economy of both nations throughout their history, before and since European colonization. Australia is made up of an island continent roughly comparable in area to the continental United States and a number of continental and offshore islands, of which the largest, Tasmania, is a state in its own right. The current population is around 20 million, mostly concentrated in the southeastern and southwestern corners and a strip of around 150 kilometers inland from the eastern coast. New Zealand (increasingly known today by its Maori name of Aotearoa) consists of two large islands with a total area about the same as Colorado and a population of 3.85 million.

Evaluation Context

An impression that stands out about the Australasian experience with evaluation is inconsistency—or, if you want to be more positive, baffling diversity. Some would characterize this diversity as irregular support of evaluation practice in Australasia, seldom remaining in place for a significant length of time. Evaluation, like employee training, has traditionally been one of the first targets for savings in the periodic economy drives that affect all levels of government at all points in the economic cycle. One obvious consequence of this cyclical behavior is that in the low periods, a radical loss of collective memory occurs. When evaluation eventually comes back, its implementation is severely handicapped by a lack of suitably skilled practitioners.

Key Characteristics of the Evaluation Environment

Amid this unevenness it is possible to identify at least three significant common characteristics of evaluation in Australia and New Zealand.

Dominant Role of Government. Not only are the great majority of programs still delivered directly by government, but even where evaluation has been required for interventions by the voluntary sector, its funding has generally been dependent on government grants.

Limited Role for Evaluation Specialists. The strong role of the government is largely responsible for the lack of a substantial specialist evaluation profession. Within government, even where there are specialist evaluation units, most people who work in them do so for only a year or two at a time, as one step in a diversified career. Outside government employment, the uncertainty of continuing demand, and the relatively low proportion of evaluations that are externally commissioned make it difficult for any consultant to survive commercially on evaluation alone.

Integration with Other Program Management Activities. This lack of a defined profession is partly the result, and partly a cause, of the third significant characteristic: strong integration of evaluation with other aspects of program performance management and accountability reporting. While the business-derived techniques of performance management (such as program budgeting, performance indicators, and output reporting) initially developed separately from evaluation, there has been a growing tendency since the mid-1990s to treat evaluation as one of a repertoire of complementary tools, often implemented through a common framework.

Opportunities and Challenges

As far as the quality of evaluation is concerned, these national characteristics lead to a distinctive pattern of incentives. Some of these favor the development of constructive evaluation practices and the use of evaluation.
These are the opportunities:

• Since most evaluation takes place within the government sector, it is easier for a central government agency to achieve coordination, strategic prioritization, and consistent standards of quality and comparability in evaluation across different programs and portfolios.

• Greater reliance on internal evaluation creates the potential for a better environment, not only for implementation of the findings but also for process use and the integration of evaluation into organizational learning processes.

• The fluid nature of the evaluation profession should in principle reduce the likelihood that evaluation will develop a guild mentality and become isolated from the living policy context.

- The absence of an entrenched, theory-dominated academic interest group reduces the risk of developing an obsessive concern with methodology at the expense of such things as contextual knowledge and relevance to the decision maker's needs.
- Integrating evaluation with other forms of performance management offers the potential to ensure that evaluation is left to do the kinds of things it does best rather than acting as a substitute for short-cycle performance monitoring.
- Integrated planning of evaluation and other performance management processes, provided it is done well, may improve the usefulness of regularly collected performance data for evaluation purposes, just as periodic evaluation can help over time to make performance information in general more relevant and reliable.
- Where boundary issues are not a significant concern, there is more latitude for self-evaluation, devolved and continuous evaluation, and various kinds of hybrid activity that serve specific information and decision needs more effectively than a rigorously separate evaluation function might.

Some national characteristics, in contrast, constitute significant risks to the development of a lasting evaluation capacity and of the climate that allows evaluation to make an optimal contribution to public policy:

- The concentration of evaluation within government means that evaluation almost always takes place in an environment that is heavily politicized by both electoral politics and the inevitable internal dynamics of any bureaucratic organization.
- Too much dependence on government for a continuing demand base leaves both the ethos of evaluation and its capacity base highly vulnerable to shifts in political priority, as well as to the inevitably recurring demands for savings in public expenditure.
- This lack of continuity limits the opportunity for a deep base of theory, skills, or practical experience in evaluation to develop within individual agencies or across the policy community as a whole. In such an environment, a heavy responsibility falls on the universities to provide a repository for collective memory and the accumulation of experience and wisdom.
- When integration is done badly, it often works against a truly evaluative culture, because evaluation becomes absorbed and ultimately submerged in a range of more routine data-gathering and reporting activities.
- In those increasingly common instances where evaluation needs to be coordinated with all the other responsibilities of a manager, often without either specific training or an additional allowance of time, it is inevitable that in many places, it will be handled cursorily, without an adequate understanding, and without the shift in mind-set that is required when moving from normal administrative or political work into evaluative work.

The Need for Standards

When a group (Rose, 2001) in AES embarked on an effort to develop a policy on standards, the Program Evaluation Standards of the Joint Committee on Standards for Educational Evaluation (1994) were the starting point. It became apparent in analyzing these standards that the requirements leading to their development depended on a number of fundamental preconditions or assumptions that did not necessarily hold true in our environment. The most important of these were:

- The core concept of an evaluation, that is, a stand-alone research exercise focused on a single program or implementation, rather than evaluation as a continuous, integral, and flexibly defined element of the public management process
- The expectation that most evaluations would be carried out externally under contract
- A confidence that most clients recognized the legitimacy of evaluation and shared a broadly common understanding of what it was and what it was useful for
- A robust and stable profession of trained specialist evaluators, with its own associated academic discipline and a reasonable level of public recognition and, potentially, political clout
- A diverse client base, including some large, securely funded nongovernmental organizations prepared to let the profession take the lead in defining professional standards and willing to support it in the process, financially and in other practical ways
- A strong interest within the profession in questions of theory and a tradition of dissension based on rival concepts of what constituted adequately rigorous and scientific techniques

The main consequence of these assumed preconditions, it seemed, was that the Program Evaluation Standards appeared to provide attention primarily to risks that were internal to the evaluation itself: risks of evaluators' overreaching themselves, overlooking key aspects of their task, exercising bias, behaving unethically, or failing to apply an appropriate range and quality of techniques.

By contrast, many of the risks requiring attention in AES were external to the evaluation process. In a workshop held at the 2001 AES conference, participants prepared a comprehensive list of the risks they felt could potentially be addressed by national standards. It is useful to reproduce that list here in order to illustrate the particular kinds of challenges that evaluation practitioners in Australia and New Zealand face (Rose, 2001):

Management Risks
- Client refusal to accept recommendations even after accepting the process
- Multiple changes to management/government

- Management changing its mind about what is required
- Culture of blame
- Confusion with personal performance assessment
- Inadequate understanding of what evaluation is
- Fear of evaluation

Evaluator Risks

- Inadequate knowledge of how to evaluate, what evaluation is, what purposes it serves
- Need for a "no-surprises" approach (cf. Audit)
- Evaluator bias (too much engagement)
- Lack of evaluator understanding of organizational culture, culture of program clients
- No standard learning path/apprenticeship

Stakeholder Risks

- Evaluation process captured by particular stakeholders
- "Professional" stakeholders [the practice among some government agencies of retaining regular community representatives or industry representatives who are automatically brought in to any consultative process (including evaluation) without properly considering in each case how representative their views actually are of the stakeholder groups in question]
- Unresponsiveness to stakeholders
- Neglected stakeholder complaints

Budget Risks

- Under-resourcing
- Budget blowouts
- Budgetary constraints on methodology
- Impact of limited budget on quality of data and confidence in report
- Not managing client expectations early enough to meet dollar constraints

Scoping Risks

- Evaluation does not address or answer the terms of reference
- Terms of reference do not address issues, but are treated as absolute
- Hidden agendas
- Outcome determined in advance
- Methodology inadequate to (or too ambitious for) scope of evaluation
- Taking on more than you can handle

Data Collection Risks

- Misplaced expectation that community organizations can provide necessary data
- Lost documentation for summative evaluation
- Data-free (or even outcome-free) programs
- Dishonest/unwilling subjects

Reporting Risks

- Temptation to talk up positives and play down negatives
- Nobody takes notice of findings (choose to ignore, don't have power to implement, don't understand them)

- No structured follow-up
- Unrealistic recommendations (not politically feasible)
- Misleading reports are a risk to the credibility of the profession

Two main aspects stand out. The first is that relatively few of the concerns have anything to do with the primary matters covered by the Program Evaluation Standards: quality of methodology, quality of data, conscientiousness, and comprehensiveness. Instead, they are primarily threats that have to do with the way evaluation is managed, planned, supported, and, above all, used. The second is that the great majority of threats lie outside the control of the individual evaluator or even of the evaluation team as a whole. Consequently, any standards, guidelines, or protocols that effectively addressed these risks would need to be observed primarily by those who commission and use evaluation.

This emphasis on questions of planning, use, and integration with the policy process runs through all the various attempts, especially in Australia, to develop guidelines and frameworks aimed at improving the quality of evaluation. Most of these have been the work of government—sometimes to coordinate practice across agencies, sometimes within a single agency. In principle, it makes sense for the government to concentrate on such controls, since it has a direct power to regulate the behavior of its own agencies.

AES also has a fundamental interest in use, stemming in large part from its membership profile and its long-term strategic direction. In the first few years of its existence, it went through considerable debate on whether its role should be to support, develop, and advocate for the profession of evaluators or the practice of evaluation. This was eventually resolved in favor of the view that its primary function should be to provide a bridge between the providers and consumers of evaluation (Trotman, 2003). This definition is reflected in the society's principal stated aim: "to improve the theory, practice and use of evaluation." It also means that the society has always encouraged users as well as practitioners to become members and attend its conferences, and has made it a key priority for its main publications (*Evaluation News and Comment* up to 2000, *Evaluation Journal of Australasia* from 2001 on) to provide articles that are accessible and informative to users and potential users as well as to scholars and practitioners.

Thus, when it was developing its policy on ethics, the AES saw it as desirable to supplement its code of practitioner ethics with a set of Guidelines for the Ethical Conduct of Evaluations, "directed to all those who *commission, prepare,* conduct *and use* evaluations. . . . They outline *procedures that might be adopted to ensure* that ethical principles are observed" (AES, 2002, p. 3, emphasis added).

It is important to recognize that these considerations are constrained by the recurring problem of limited capacity. The Program Evaluation Standards appear to start from a presumption that most people who go into evaluation will have a reasonably clear idea of what evaluation is, what it is for, and how it is done. No such presumption can safely be made in Australia or New Zealand.

Two Problems and a Practical Constraint

These distinctive requirements pose two major problems for any professional body trying to develop standards for evaluation and obtain widespread support for their implementation. First, given that the government has the authority and motivation to impose its own internal quality controls on evaluation, there is much less argument for the profession to carry out that role. Yet the problem remains that the commitment of the government to observe good standards can be guaranteed only as long as political support for evaluation remains in place.

The second difficulty is that an emphasis on practicality requires extremely specific and tangible guidelines, yet the practice of evaluation in Australia and the kinds of context in which it is carried out vary widely. In reality, the resources available are very finite indeed, and herein lies the most important practical constraint. The development of standards requires an enormous commitment of time, experience, and dedication, often over many years. The AES is a relatively small body, with its membership fluctuating between 600 and 700 over the past five years; however, this aggregate figure is misleading because the turnover in membership is high. The chances of finding the critical mass of committed volunteers from within its membership is slight at the best of times and tends to decline as increasing fiscal stringency leads to evaluation units' becoming more overloaded.

These demands must be seen in the light of the fact that the AES is struggling to offer a full set of professional development activities. The shortage of practitioners with a long, continuous experience in evaluation reduces the likelihood that the required expertise will be available among the society's membership.

Development of Standards: The Story So Far

It would be unfair to concentrate on the efforts of AES without first acknowledging the progress that has been made by governments. A number of states in the 1970s and 1980s put considerable effort into developing guidelines and frameworks to encourage quality evaluation, often employing the most respected evaluation practitioners as advisers. Individual agencies have also chalked up achievements in this area, among the more recent being the Victorian Department of Primary Industry and the commonwealth agency Centrelink (whose mandate is confined to delivering programs developed elsewhere; hence, it has no policy function). The development since 2001 of a new national framework for the delivery of natural resource management programs has also included agreement on a sophisticated monitoring and evaluation framework, which is one of the first of its kind anywhere to be built around a core of program logic with a particular emphasis on surfacing and testing the assumptions behind each intervention (www. deh.gov.au/nrm/monitoring/evn/pubs/me.framework.pdf).

On a whole-of-government scale, one of the most noteworthy contributions was that of the Australian National Audit Office (ANAO), which carried out a major review in 1995 and 1996 of the experience of mandatory evaluation as implemented by the commonwealth. One of the products of this performance audit was the formulation of a set of Better Practice Principles, concerned primarily with the effective planning and management of evaluation and its integration into ongoing program management and policy development. This document (Australian National Audit Office, 1997) set out twenty-five recommended practices under four main headings:

- Approaches to Evaluation Planning
- Conduct of Individual Evaluations
- Quality of Evaluation Reports
- Impact of Evaluations

Had these principles become better known and been effectively enforced, it is possible they would have mitigated many of the failings identified by the audit in the implementation of the mandatory evaluation framework. Regrettably, they were defeated by bad timing. The ANAO, though it maintains a watching brief over the evaluation activity of agencies through its program of performance audits, has no recognized authority to administer such guidelines or standards.

In more recent years, the lead in this area seems to have passed to New Zealand. Recent central agency reviews, such as the *Review of the Centre* (Advisory Group for the Review of the Centre, 2001) and the more specific review of evaluative activity in government carried out in 2003 by the Treasury and the State Services Commission (Ryan, 2003), offer the promise of a structured whole-of-government approach, giving a balanced emphasis to issues of quality and use.

The second of the needs identified above (for practical guidance to bridge the recurring capacity gaps) was one the AES chose to handle by alternative means. Rather than attempting to enshrine good practice in standards, it instituted a process in 1996 to develop a comprehensive set of evaluation competencies. A working party made up jointly of practitioners and academics carried out this work, taking some five years to produce a set of detailed recommendations (English, Cummings, Funnell, and Kaleveld, 2002).

However, discussion of standards continued sporadically in the background through the 1990s. Three competing views developed:

- The Program Evaluation Standards were an adequate guide so far as they went; where they failed to cover a situation, Australasian evaluators could have recourse to other relevant professional or organizational codes.
- The Program Evaluation Standards would serve the purpose provided they were amplified with explanatory notes on their local application or modified in aspects of detail.
- It would be more productive, while taking the Program Evaluation Standards as a starting point, to go through a formal process of developing a specific set of Australasian standards, partly for the sake of the greater interest and involvement in quality issues that would be generated among members by the development process.

Unfortunately, other demands on the time of the committee members meant that progress on the adaptation of the Program Evaluation Standards was much slower than originally desired, and the most important product, other than the preliminary discussion paper (Fraser, 2001a), was a draft set of standards presented for discussion at a workshop at the 2001 conference. (This document was never published, but I am happy to supply an electronic copy on request to interested readers.)

Considerations of space preclude a detailed discussion of this draft. Briefly, in an attempt to address the tension between keeping the document to a manageable size and providing enough guidance to cover a representative range of real situations, it followed the example of the Program Evaluation Standards by setting six ruling standards judged to be applicable in all reasonably foreseeable circumstances, with each ruling standard generating a number of more specific and more practically focused subsidiary standards (see Table 6.1).

Comparing this list with the number of standards in each category in the Program Evaluation Standards should make it clear not only that the draft Australasian standards were considerably more numerous and detailed, but also how the balance of emphasis differs between the two documents. Note in particular how transparency, an issue that does not rate its own separate category in the Program Evaluation Standards, is one of the three largest categories in this draft, while "accuracy, quality, and comprehensiveness" make up a far smaller proportion of the overall total of standards, and "ethics" requires considerably less articulation, largely because AES already had a comprehensive code of practitioner ethics in place.

No real agreement emerged from the workshop on the proper future course of action. If there was a common viewpoint, it was probably that we should continue to treat the Program Evaluation Standards as a source of general guidance where applicable, without attempting to adhere slavishly to them and without necessarily precluding further work of our own. Although the Ethics and Standards Committee is continuing to explore opportunities for further development work, possibly on a more modest scale, no significant progress has been made since 2001.

Table 6.1. The Ruling Standards

Transparency (ten subsidiary standards)	Evaluation should promote the widest possible awareness and understanding. Hence, it must be honest and open in its processes and in the way it reports its findings.
Utility (fifteen standards)	Evaluation should effectively support knowledge-driven decision making and facilitate learning in organizations, governments, and the wider community.
Practicality (seven standards)	Evaluations should be planned and resourced in such a way that it will be possible with normal effort to complete them in the time available and to the standard required.
Cost-effectiveness (one standard)	Evaluation should be planned and carried out in such a way as to produce the most useful and informative results that are possible within the constraints of the time and resources available.
Ethics (seven standards)	Evaluation should be carried out with fairness, probity, and professionalism and with respect for the rights, welfare, and sensitivities of all parties involved and affected.
Accuracy, quality, and comprehensiveness (twelve standards)	Evaluation should be based on comprehensive, sound, balanced, and defensible information, having regard to the purposes that each individual evaluation activity is required to serve.

Future Prospects

While further work on standards remains on the agenda of the AES board, it is difficult to be optimistic about progress in the short term. If Australia and New Zealand choose to develop standards in the conventionally accepted sense, "ruling standards" may be the best approach. However, in the light of developments internationally, it seems more likely that attention will shift to alternative means of covering the same needs.

One possibility that may warrant consideration is that instead of trying to set rules that others can follow or not at their discretion, it might be more useful to prepare a series of short guides, giving a basic set of guidelines to people who are being required to carry out or organize evaluation for the first time on such basic matters as how to set up an evaluation strategy, how much work is involved in an evaluation, what sort of budget is realistic, and what outcomes can reasonably be accepted for a given level of effort. It seems likely that the AES would carry more credibility in the general policy community as a source of such expert advice than if it were to try to impose its values and criteria (even supposing it can agree on what they are) on organizations that have no compelling incentive to follow its lead.

The other potential for the development of standards comes from an unanticipated quarter. For several years, the AES has had the question of evaluation by and for indigenous communities at the top of its strategic agenda. Particularly in New Zealand, where there is a strong Maori presence in both the evaluation community and the program client population, there are increasing demands from Maori to adapt practice to their cultural norms and needs, so that evaluation can better serve their social and cultural requirements. This push comes in part from increasingly shared concerns that evaluation (even when done with Maori participation) risks becoming a rationalization for the values and economic priorities of the dominant culture. Work is already proceeding to develop culturally relevant quality standards in a number of New Zealand's social research institutions, with the effort spreading out to other Polynesian and Pacific nations.

Although it may be some time before this initiative gains sufficient impetus to spread to Australia, it certainly appears at this stage to be one area in which there is a sufficient base of passion and commitment to drive the kind of sustained, intensive process required before there can be any substantial achievement in the area of standards.

References

Advisory Group for the Review of the Centre. *Review of the Centre.* 2001. [www.executive.govt.nz/minister/mallard/ssc/review_of_centre.pdf].

Australasian Evaluation Society. *Guidelines for the Ethical Conduct of Evaluations.* 2002. [www.aes.asn.au].

Australian National Audit Office. "Program Evaluation in the Australian Public Service: Audit Report No. 3, 1997–98." Canberra: Commonwealth of Australia, 1997. [http://www.anao.gov.au/WebSite.nsf/Publications/4A256AE90015F69B4A256905000 98A73].

English, B., Cummings, R., Funnell, S., and Kaleveld, E. "Competencies for Evaluation Practitioners: Where to from Here?" *Evaluation Journal of Australasia,* 2002, 2(2), 13–15.

Fraser, D. "Beyond Ethics: Why We Need Evaluation Standards." *Evaluation Journal of Australasia,* 2001a, 1(1), 53–58.

Fraser, D. "Development of AES standards." *Evaluation Journal of Australasia,* 2001b, 1(1), 59.

Joint Committee on Standards for Educational Evaluation. *Program Evaluation Standards.* (2nd ed.) Thousand Oaks, Calif.: Sage, 1994.

Lunt, N., and Trotman, I. G. "A Stagecraft of New Zealand Evaluation." *Evaluation Journal of Australasia,* forthcoming.

Rose, K. "Workshop on AES Standards Development Held on 11 October 2001." *Evaluation Journal of Australasia,* 2001, 1(2), 49–51.

Ryan, B. "'Death by Evaluation?' Reflections on Monitoring and Evaluation in Australia and New Zealand." *Evaluation Journal of Australasia,* 2003, 3(1), 6–16.

Sharp, C. A. "Development of Program Evaluation in Australia and the Australasian Evaluation Society—the Early Decades." *Evaluation Journal of Australasia,* 3(2), 2003.

Trotman, I. G. "Reflections on a Decade in the Life of the Australasian Evaluation Society—1990–1999." *Evaluation Journal of Australasia,* 3(2), 2003.

DOUG FRASER is a freelance evaluation and policy consultant working out of Hobart, Tasmania.

In describing the efforts of CARE International, this chapter demonstrates how nongovernmental organizations have begun to set their own evaluation standards.

The CARE International Evaluation Standards

Jim Rugh

The 1996 American Evaluation Association conference in Atlanta featured a session on strategies to promote monitoring and evaluation (M&E) in international nongovernmental organizations (INGOs). At that time, there was a lengthy list of proposed initiatives to be undertaken in CARE. With the perspective of hindsight and reviewing the achievements of the past eight years, CARE believes that the strategy that had the most significant impact on strengthening the quality of its program development, monitoring, and evaluation was the creation of a set of standards. The implementation of the standards as well as their development are also viewed as important. This is the story of that process, told by the person who led the effort.

CARE International is one of the world's largest independent global relief and development organizations. The organization operates in over 72 countries in Asia, Africa, Latin America, the Middle East, and Eastern Europe. CARE's 11 offices in Europe, Australia, North America, and Japan are independent nonprofit organizations. These offices contribute to and help manage over 750 projects around the world that benefit over 45 million people every year. The United Nations, World Bank, the European Union, USAID, and the British government all support CARE's global programs. CARE maintains a staff rich in diversity. Out of more than 12,000 employees, over 11,000 are nationals of the countries where CARE conducts programs (CARE UK, 2004).

CARE's Vision and Mission

CARE's vision is for "a world of hope, tolerance, and social justice, where poverty has been overcome and people live in dignity and security. CARE International will be a global force and partner of choice within a worldwide movement dedicated to ending poverty. CARE will be known everywhere for its unshakeable commitment to the dignity of people" (CARE International, 2003a, p. 1). Its mission is "to serve individuals and families in the poorest communities in the world. Drawing strength from its global diversity, resources, and experience, CARE promotes innovative solutions and advocates for global responsibility. The organization facilitates lasting change by strengthening capacity for self-help, providing economic opportunity, delivering relief in emergencies, influencing policy decisions at all levels, and addressing discrimination in all its forms. Guided by the aspirations of local communities, CARE pursues its mission with both excellence and compassion because the people whom CARE serves deserve nothing less" (CARE International, 2003a, p. 2).

Programming Principles and Sectors

In order to complete its mission, CARE conforms to six programming principles (CARE International, 2003a):

1. CARE promotes empowerment by standing in solidarity with poor and marginalized people and supports their efforts to take control of their own lives and fulfill their rights.
2. CARE works with partners to maximize the impact of its programs.
3. CARE seeks ways to be held accountable to the poor and marginalized people whom it serves.
4. CARE addresses discrimination on the basis of sex, race, nationality, ethnicity, class, religion, age, physical ability, caste, opinion, or sexual orientation in its programs and offices.
5. CARE promotes the nonviolent resolution of conflicts.
6. CARE seeks sustainable results by addressing the underlying causes of poverty and rights denial.

CARE creates projects that conform to these principles in eight sectors (CARE Secretariat, 2004):

• Emergency relief: CARE can quickly assess a disaster situation and offer an integrated solution that realizes the long-term development needs of the community. For short-term relief, CARE provides food, temporary shelter, clean water, and other essentials to victims of regional conflicts or natural disasters.

• Conservation and environment: This sector deals with projects in environmentally sensitive areas such as endangered rain forests and some of the highly cultivated regions in the Andes and Himalayas.

• Agriculture: CARE helps farmers adopt new measures to grow and sell crops for a higher profit without using harmful pesticides or dangerous equipment.

• Education and training: CARE provides training to local individuals and families, especially to girls and women, so they will possess skills to make better decisions within their own communities.

• Small business support: CARE frees people from poverty by providing small loans, business training, and technical assistance.

• Gender development: CARE works to involve women as project participants, decision makers, and beneficiaries. CARE also focuses on women's issues such as reproductive health, family planning, income generation, and girls' education.

• Primary health care: Constructing wells, immunizing children, teaching mothers how to prevent diseases, and providing nourishing food to poor families are projects in CARE's health sector to combat child mortality.

• Rehabilitation: After a humanitarian disaster, CARE International maintains a long-term commitment to the different communities with which it works.

By conducting projects in these eight sectors in nations all over the world, CARE International continues its dedication to aiding people in dire situations and poverty.

Design, Monitoring, and Evaluation Unit

Over the past decade, CARE has placed increasing emphasis on improving program quality through better holistic program design, systematic monitoring, and credible evaluation practice (Goldenberg, 2003). In 1995, it created the Design, Monitoring, and Evaluation (DME) Unit and named me to head the operation. The unit coordinates the work of a cadre of CARE staff around the world who have direct or indirect responsibilities for promoting good project design, developing and implementing systematic monitoring systems, and planning for and conducting evaluations that are credible and useful. Workshops have been held in West and East Africa, Latin America, the Middle East, and Asia aimed at increasing linkages among countries and programs, developing a worldwide DME cadre, and building capacity (CARE Partnership and Household Livelihood Security, 2004). More recently, CARE has developed principles, standards, and guidelines for ensuring the quality of DME now in use by CARE members, country offices, sectors, and projects around the world.

The DME Standards

In response to a request by senior management that DME report on how many projects have achieved impact, DME undertook a major evaluation initiative. It wanted to clarify the definition of *impact* and what it takes to design for, achieve, and measure it. DME also wanted to use metaevaluations to determine how successful the projects were. This became an evolving, multiyear undertaking called the Impact Evaluation Initiative (IEI).

The process began by asking regional managers to identify which of the projects in their countries showed the best prospects for achieving and measuring impact. In other words, the initiative began by looking for the "positive deviants" to see what could be learned from them as models of best practice. Eventually managers identified nine projects in nine different countries. A consultant was asked to review documents describing these projects, including project proposals, monitoring and evaluation plans, and any evaluations that had taken place. Case studies were written on each of these projects, summarizing the main attributes, strengths, weaknesses, and experiences of each. From these case studies, an initial list of best practices was drafted.

Representatives of those projects and country offices were invited to the first IEI workshop in Atlanta in April 1999 (CARE USA, 2001). Using the case studies that had been prepared, participants generated a checklist of guidelines for the DME processes. The next phase of the initiative was to develop an instrument to help project staff assess themselves against the impact evaluation checklist. The DME Capacity Assessment Toolkit (DME CAT) includes a sixteen-page discussion guide and questionnaire to which project staff respond, preferably facilitated by an outsider to add objectivity. The DME CAT packet also includes a self-assessment questionnaire to ascertain individual skills and needs for training in DME and another questionnaire addressing CARE country office systems. The second questionnaire includes an examination of roles and responsibilities related to DME. This assessment packet was accompanied by extensive training workshops to help staff understand the standards. The following comment from one participant was representative of comments received from several others: "This process was not only an assessment of our DME capacity; it was capacity development itself."

Because there was a mandate from senior management that all country offices and projects go through the DME CAT assessment process, 186 projects in 23 countries completed the exercise in a two-year period. Based on the feedback received, they did this not only because they were told to. Many also expressed appreciation for the clarity provided by DME practice and its contribution to program quality and impact. There were many stories of how this checklist helped project staff consider dimensions not previously realized in project design and monitoring and evaluation systems. The results of the DME CAT assessments were summarized in the

CARE DME Capacity Assessment Global Synthesis Report (Johri, 2002). According to the report's author,

> In putting it all together what is strikingly evident is the discord in the process from Design to Monitoring to Evaluation. The leap of faith from the "D" to the "M&E" of projects is occasioned by, on the one hand, having rich technical inputs at the proposal development stage through the Sector Coordinators and Project Managers. On the other hand, detailed M&E plans exist for only 45% of projects. There is divided responsibility of DME. The resulting ad hoc monitoring and evaluation systems then "respond to key questions formulated by those involved, not to an evaluation plan written during the design phase" (comment from CARE-Bolivia). Though 65% of projects said their staff was measuring outcomes, one wonders if they are actually involved in evaluating the loftier goals of the projects [Johri, 2002, p. iii].

The second IEI Conference (IEI-II) was held in England in 2001 (CARE USA, 2001). The conference was structured around plenary presentations and facilitated by small groups called dialogue teams. The teams reported to the plenary, followed by discussion. Results were presented from DME capacity assessments of 186 projects in 23 country offices. After presentations, participants considered the implications for the DME Standards and Guidelines of CARE's evolving programming lenses: Household Livelihood Security, the Rights Based Approaches, Partnership and Civil Society, and Gender Equity and Diversity. Participants also had the opportunity to reflect on the implications of different forms of intervention, varying donor orientations, and country office alignment patterns within the CARE system. The conference produced, among other things, a revised set of proposed CARE International DME Standards that were recommended to and later adopted by the CARE International Program Working Group and then the CARE International Board (Exhibit 7.1).

Application of CARE's DME Standards

The introduction to the DME standards provides some guidance for their application. It states:

> These CARE standards apply to all CARE programming (including emergencies, rehabilitation and development) and all forms of interventions (direct service delivery, working with or through partners, and policy advocacy).
>
> These standards, as well as accompanying guidelines, should be used to: guide the work of project designers; as a checklist for approval of project proposals; as a tool for periodic project self-appraisal; and as a part of project evaluation. The emphasis should not be only on enforcement but also on the strengthening of capacity to be able to meet these standards for program

Exhibit 7.1. Official CARE Standards

1. Be consistent with the CARE International Vision and Mission and Programming Principles. Projects and programs should fit comfortably within the spirit and content of the CARE International (CI) vision and mission statements. In other words, CARE projects should show how they will contribute, ultimately, towards lasting improvements in human well-being, hope, tolerance, social justice, reduction in poverty, and the enhanced dignity and security of people. They should be guided by CI programming principles that synthesize and integrate central elements of CARE's evolving program approaches, including livelihoods, basic rights, gender and diversity, partnerships, and civil society.

2. Be clearly linked to a country office strategy and/or long-term program goal. Projects should not be isolated, but they should be clearly embedded in long-term multi-project programs and strategic frameworks that address the underlying conditions and root causes of poverty and social injustice. Doing so provides a larger framework in which project decisions are made, but it does not preclude strategic innovation and experimentation. CARE's strategies should be clearly linked to the development efforts of others, such as government, multilaterals, and NGOs.

3. Ensure the active participation and influence of stakeholders in its analysis, design, implementation, monitoring, and evaluation processes. Every project should be explicit about its process of participation and consultation, aiming for openness and transparency. "Stakeholder" will be understood to include target communities, partner organizations, governments, and CARE staff. The interventions of the various actors should be coordinated and reinforcing. Individually and together, they must work to achieve sustainable impact.

4. Have a design that is based on a holistic analysis of the needs and rights of the target populations and the underlying causes of their conditions of poverty and social injustice. It should also examine the opportunities and risks inherent in the potential interventions. The diagnostic assessment and subsequent analysis should be based on a clear frame of reference and include an analysis of problems and their causes from a range of perspectives, including institutional as well as opportunity analysis. Social analyses could examine how needs and rights are related to gender, social class, ethnicity, and religion. The analysis should lead to an understanding of institutional capacity, power relationships, and the exercise of rights and responsibilities, as well as household level conditions.

5. Use a logical framework that explains how the project will ultimately impact the lives of members of a defined target population. The project plan should be clearly summarized in a logic model that shows how proposed interventions and anticipated outputs will result in defined effects and impact. It should specify the level of intervention, such as household, community, institutional, and societal levels. The plan should tell how the project would ultimately contribute to sustainable impact for a specific target population. It should also identify key assumptions and provide validation for its central hypothesis.

6. Set a significant yet achievable and measurable final goal. A project final goal must be achievable and measurable during the life of the project. This calls for project designers to clearly define what the project will be held accountable for achieving. It should be practical and doable, yet it should be at the outcome level, which is intermediary impact or at least effect, rather than output level.

   A project final goal must also be clearly linked and significantly contribute to "higher-level" program or strategic goals. Program goals should address underlying causes of poverty and social injustice, but their impact, "equitable and durable improvements in human wellbeing and social justice," should be ultimately manifest at the household or individual level.

Exhibit 7.1. Official CARE Standards (*continued*)

7. Be technically, environmentally, and socially appropriate. Interventions should be based on best current practice and on an understanding of the social context and the needs, rights, and responsibilities of the stakeholders. The project must be designed in a way that is likely to make a significant and positive difference, with minimal undesired social or environmental consequences. Interventions must make reference to technical or sectoral experience or standards, developed by CARE or others, to demonstrate the viability of their approach. Environmental analysis could include assessment of current status, analysis of potential impact, and regional environmental issues. These may require technical appraisal by those with expertise in the relevant professions.

8. Indicate the appropriateness of project costs in light of the selected project strategies and expected outputs and outcomes. Program designers must be able to defend the budget of a project relative to its outputs, scale, and anticipated impact. Also, the M&E plan should include methods for measuring cost effectiveness, i.e., to demonstrate that the costs of project interventions are reasonable and commensurate with the outputs and outcomes achieved.

9. Develop and implement a monitoring and evaluation plan and system based on the logical framework that ensures the collection of baseline, monitoring, and final evaluation data. It should anticipate how the information would be used for decision making. Its budget must be an adequate amount for implementing the monitoring and evaluation plan. M&E plans should provide sufficient detail to clearly identify evaluation design, sources of data, means of measurement, schedule for measurement, data processing and analysis, dissemination of information to and utilization by key stakeholders, and responsibilities for each of these processes. A sufficient budget should be allocated for designated tasks, and planning should ensure that CARE staff and partners have the capacity required for their implementation. Monitoring information should be useful and timely for promoting reflective practice, management decision making, and adapting project approaches and strategies. M&E plans should incorporate methods to measure risks and assumptions and to track unintended effects.

10. Establish a baseline for measuring change in indicators of impact and effect by conducting a study or survey prior to implementation of project activities. There needs to be a distinction between a diagnostic assessment and a baseline study. The former gathers a little information about many conditions and is used to inform project design. A baseline study, on the other hand, should focus on measuring indicators of effect and impact with a level of rigor required for a "before-and-after" comparison with evaluation. Baseline studies can use qualitative as well as quantitative data, as long as they describe the initial situation with sufficient precision to be able to clearly measure changes over the project's life.

11. Use indicators that are relevant, measurable, verifiable, and reliable. Indicators should be capable of yielding data that can be disaggregated to the individual level according to criteria that reveal vulnerabilities such as gender, age, and social class. Both qualitative and quantitative measures are acceptable as long as they can illustrate discernible and significant change. For indicators to be reliable denotes that they are robust, useful, and credible throughout the life of the project. CARE should draw upon the international development community's great wealth of experience with indicators.

Exhibit 7.1. Official CARE Standards (*continued*)

12. Employ a balance of evaluation methodologies, assure an appropriate level of rigor, and adhere to recognized standards. Evaluation should be incorporated as standard practice as a basis for accountability and for documented, institutionalized learning. Although various forms of evaluation should be planned, such as internal or external, formative (midterm) or summative (final), or even ex post (to evaluate sustainability), the minimum is that there should be at least a final evaluation that summarizes the achievements and lessons learned by the project.

    Diagnostic assessments, baseline studies, monitoring, and evaluations should use a balance of methodological approaches to ensure triangulation, a richness of data, and mutual modifications. Evaluations should assure appropriate levels of rigor and precision in their designs and selection of methodologies. Informant confidentiality should be protected. Each evaluation event should draw upon previous ones and anticipate subsequent events. Evaluation processes must be documented and carefully archived, allowing subsequent project phases to replicate methods and draw upon comparative data.

13. Be informed by and contribute to ongoing learning within and outside CARE. It is critical that relevant research and previous project evaluations inform the initial proposal preparation state. Furthermore, learning should also apply throughout the life of a project and beyond. The lessons learned from a project should be adequately documented for use in the design of other projects. Project management should support the documentation of project processes, including redesigns. Reflective practice, such as the regular use of monitoring data, should be built into every project. Learning should be an organization-wide priority supported by frequent meta-evaluations.

Source: CARE International (2003b, p. 612).

quality. At the time of initial approval, if a project can not meet one or more standards, there should be an explanation of why and what will be done about it. More than a "passed/failed" checklist, this calls for a description of how well a project meets each standard and an action plan for how it will better meet these standards going forward [CARE International, 2003b, p. 1].

Application of the DME standards is operationalized through the Project Standards Measurement Instrument (PSMI), which uses a combination of qualitative and quantitative methods to help project staff understand the standards and assess how well their project currently meets them (CARE International, 2003b). A Likert score is included on the PSMI for each standard. The staff gains value from the process by recording responses to the questions, for example, describing how a project is involving participants, noting strengths and weaknesses, and using the findings to generate an action plan for further strengthening program quality in the future.

CARE's standards do not focus only on evaluations. This is because they were developed as part of a process for enhancing the quality of project design and implementation, or monitoring, not only as an external evaluative function of judging projects after they have been completed. As one manager put it, "It doesn't help us very much to be told by the evaluator that our project failed. We'd rather be helped to plan for and undertake projects in ways that lead to successful outcomes." Thus, the CARE project DME standards are used to ascertain the adequacy of initial design for periodic self-assessment. This leads to enhanced quality as a project matures, as well as a part of a summative evaluation.

Assessing CARE's Impact

In response to questions by senior management, CARE conducted a meta-evaluation of goal achievement (MEGA) in 2000 (Goldenberg, 2001). It consisted of a review of 104 evaluation documents, primarily final project evaluations, written between 1994 and 2000. It not only looked for measurement of impact but it also examined the methodologies used for such measurement. The Joint Committee on Standards for Educational Evaluation (1994) recommends applying the Program Evaluation Standards to a report as a way of conducting a metaevaluation. One might have expected the CARE DME standards to be used in a similar manner. However, the evaluator who conducted the MEGA metaevaluation did not apply either the Joint Committee standards or the CARE DME standards. Instead, he reviewed each document and recorded key characteristics in a series of tables covering goals, objectives, and findings; lessons learned, partnership comments, and sustainability findings; evaluation rigor and range of methods; and a broad range of methodology and topical characteristics.

The metaevaluation found that most CARE projects had a significant impact on the lives of people in poor communities. The survey found that 66 percent of CARE's projects achieved most of their objectives, and an additional 29 percent achieved at least some objectives. Only 5 percent showed no substantial results. These findings were consistent across all sectors. The CARE USA board, the CARE International Program Working Group, and other major stakeholders were so pleased with the first MEGA report that they asked for its repetition every two years.

The second MEGA, conducted in 2002 and using the same procedure, consisted of a review of 65 evaluation documents, primarily final project evaluations (Goldenberg, 2003). Almost all of them were written between 2000 and 2002. Whereas MEGA'00 had relied on a review of both abstracts and original documents, MEGA'02 was based entirely on original report documents. The overwhelming majority, 82 percent of the evaluations covered by the MEGA'02, reported that projects had achieved most of their intermediate objectives. Only 18 percent demonstrated mixed results, and none were rated as having no substantial results. Even more striking was the fact that 94 percent of final evaluations reported the achievement of most project objectives. The most significant improvement over the MEGA'00 findings was the degree to which evaluations measured final goal achievement. Eighty-nine percent of the MEGA'02 evaluations did so versus only

47 percent of those in MEGA'00. Furthermore, all MEGA'02 projects were deemed to have "measurable final goals." The external evaluator who conducted the MEGA meta-evaluation synthesis did note, however, that CARE may need a more systematic manner of judging whether project objectives were achieved.

Conclusion

From my perspective as DME head, it seems that three things—the process through which the project DME standards were developed in CARE, the relevance of the content of the standards themselves, and the mainstreaming of their use throughout the 72 nation CARE consortium—have made a major impact on both the image and the reality of program quality and effectiveness. I hope that this impact translates into CARE's being better able to fulfill its mission of service to individuals and families in the poorest communities in the world.

References

CARE International. *CI Program Standards Framework.* Atlanta, Ga.: CARE International, 2003a.

CARE International. *Project Standards Measurement Instrument.* Atlanta, Ga.: CARE International, 2003b.

CARE Partnership and Household Livelihood Security. "PHLS Partnership and Household Livelihood Security: Design, Monitoring, and Evaluation." 2004. [http://www.kcenter.com/phls/dme.htm].

CARE Secretariat. "CARE's Work." 2004. [www.care-international.org/careswork.html].

CARE UK. "About CARE: CARE International." 2004. [www.careinternational.org.uk/about/careinternational.htm].

CARE USA. *Impact Evaluation Initiative II Conference Report.* Atlanta, Ga.: CARE USA, 2001.

Goldenberg, D. *The MEGA Evaluation: A Review of Findings and Methodological Lessons from CARE Final Evaluations, 1994–2000.* Atlanta, Ga.: CARE USA Program Division, 2001.

Goldenberg, D. *The MEGA 2002 Evaluation: A Review of Findings and Methodological Lessons from CARE Final Evaluations, 2001–2002.* Atlanta, Ga.: CARE USA Program Division, 2003.

Johri, N. *Design, Monitoring, and Evaluation Capacity Assessment Global Synthesis Report.* Atlanta, Ga.: CARE-USA, 2002.

Joint Committee on Standards for Educational Evaluation. *Program Evaluation Standards.* (2nd ed.) Thousand Oaks, Calif.: Sage, 1994.

JIM RUGH is coordinator of program design, monitoring, and evaluation for CARE International. He is based in Atlanta, Georgia.

8

This summary chapter reports the results of an informal analysis of the previous chapters to frame issues that the evaluation community needs to address as the global standards movement continues.

Cross-Cutting Issues in International Standards Development

Craig Russon

This issue has presented seven previous chapters on international program evaluation standards. Chapter One defined terms and identified major themes. Subsequent chapters examined evaluation standards created in North America, Europe, and Africa; those contemplated in Australasia; and the evaluation standards created by the European Commission and CARE International. This chapter summarizes three broad issues that cut across these other chapters and discusses implications for the continuing development of program evaluation standards in an international context.

Development of Standards

One of the most important findings to emerge from the informal analysis is that there has been a proliferation of evaluation standards. From 1981 until 1999, the Joint Committee's Program Evaluation Standards (1994) were the only national evaluation standards in existence. The Swiss completed the first set of national evaluation standards to be developed outside the United States and Canada in 1999. Shortly after, other regional and national evaluation organizations began developing evaluation standards of their own. This was in addition to the evaluation standards developed by governments and nongovernmental organizations.

Analysis of the chapters reveals that the standard-setting process was more or less the same for all organizations. The Joint Committee created its standards in collaboration with twelve national professional organizations. The regional and national evaluation organizations in Africa, Australasia, France, Germany, Switzerland, and the United Kingdom all named special committees to undertake standards-setting efforts. CARE International brought regional managers and country office representatives together in the Impact Evaluation Initiative. The evaluation standard-setting process seems most effective when it is public, participatory, open, and consensual.

It is interesting to note that the standard-setting efforts undertaken by regional and national evaluation organizations most often resulted in documents that were approved and endorsed by the respective organizations. The Program Evaluation Standards, which were not initiated by the national evaluation organizations of the United States or Canada, have never actually been endorsed by these bodies; instead, the American Evaluation Association and the Canadian Evaluation Society sponsor the Program Evaluation Standards.

It is undeniable that the Joint Committee's Program Evaluation Standards have had a direct and indirect influence on many other efforts to develop standards. Direct influence was evidenced when regional and national evaluation organizations used the Joint Committee's work as a point of departure for their own standard-setting efforts. (The international evaluation community owes both the Joint Committee and Sage Publications collective thanks for their willingness to support these efforts by freely allowing the use and alteration of the existing standards.) Efforts that used the Program Evaluation Standards as their point of departure have similar domains of intended audiences, and their standards are organized in a similar manner. This organization of standards has proven to be robust and sustainable even with the modification of specific standards.

The Joint Committee's work has also had an indirect influence on efforts to develop standards that did not use the Program Evaluation Standards as a point of departure. This would include several European countries, CARE International, and some national governments. When these organizations developed their standards, they used the Program Evaluation Standards as an example of what they did *not* want their standards to be.

Some national evaluation organizations, notably those in Australasia, and presumably the United Kingdom and France, and CARE International, identified what they perceived to be a limitation of the North American evaluation standards. Their critique is that the Program Evaluation Standards are aimed more at small problems than large ones. So, for example, there is a standard for identifying stakeholders, but not for prohibiting the gross distortion and misuse of evaluation, especially in developing countries. For this reason, the domains of intended audiences and the organization of these standards are different.

Implementation and Use of Standards

There has been a proliferation of evaluation standards. These standards fall into two categories: voluntary and compulsory standards. The standards put forward by regional and national evaluation organizations described in this issue are all voluntary. There is evidence to suggest that these voluntary standards have not yet met their full potential. According to Rouge (see Chapter Five, this volume), implementation and use of the African Evaluation Guidelines is a challenge. The Société française d'évaluation charter and the U.K. Evaluation Society good practice guidelines are new and have not been fully implemented. In Australasia, one of the key factors that has impeded the development of standards has been a lack of confidence that the national evaluation society has sufficient influence to secure their implementation.

The standards put forward by nongovernmental organizations and government described in this issue are all compulsory. For example, Beywl and Speer wrote in Chapter Four about the different standards that the European Commission applies to the projects that it funds. Fraser notes in Chapter Six that in Australia, governments have so far been much more influential than the profession in implementing various kinds of quality control. Rugh reports in Chapter Seven that the Design, Monitoring, and Evaluation standards apply to all CARE programs. The voluntary or compulsory distinction may ultimately have implications for which standards survive in the natural selection process that is part of the evolution of standards. The standards that are applied and used the most will endure the longest.

Yarbrough, Shuhla, and Caruthers in Chapter Two, Widmer in Chapter Three, and Bewyl and Speer in Chapter Four all reported on efforts to use evaluation standards outside the region where they were developed. At one time, this may have been appropriate and even desirable. Application of the Program Evaluation Standards outside North America certainly helped to raise international awareness about the subject. However, there are two reasons that this may no longer be appropriate: first, such use may reduce the demand for locally developed evaluation standards, and second, if such use occurs in a region or country that has developed its own evaluation standards, it could engender competition between the two sets of standards.

It appears that with a bit of modification, the three main types of evaluation use (instrumental, conceptual, and symbolic) identified in the professional literature can be applied to standards (Russon, 2003). Instrumental use occurs when standards are used to facilitate the immediate implementation of an evaluation report—for example, the use of the Swiss Evaluation Standards for meta-evaluation, guide to practice, quality assurance, and teaching aids (see Chapter Three). Conceptual use occurs when standards alter the way that stakeholders think about the object of the evaluation. The use of the Program Evaluation Standards as a conceptual structure in several books is an example (see Chapter Two). Finally, symbolic use occurs when standards shape the political purposes for which an evaluation is used (for example, to muster support for a project). The metaevaluation of goal achievement evaluations that were conducted by CARE International are examples of this type of use (see Chapter Seven, this issue).

Framing Concepts for Evaluation Standards

Two framing concepts were presented in the introductory chapter: universal standards and open standards. The argument for universal standards is that they are needed to maintain the quality of evaluations of international trade policies, migration, intellectual property, private finance, and the environment. Universal evaluation standards could facilitate the global expansion of the evaluation profession provided that they are designed to reflect the multiplicity of national and transnational contexts within which evaluation will be called on to operate.

However, if we accept Taut's premise (2000) that evaluation standards are based on the values of the culture in which they are developed, several difficult questions emerge: On whose values would universal evaluation standards be based? Is it possible to develop universal evaluation standards that would accommodate every unique cultural context without being so general that they lose all meaning? And even if we could, would we want evaluations to be judged by standards based on values far removed from the contexts in which studies are conducted?

The argument for open standards is that they eliminate the necessity of reinventing the wheel by identifying and modifying existing standards to fit different values, cultural realities, and approaches to evaluation. This creates the opportunity for evaluators to strengthen the quality of their evaluations and their ability to meet the diverse needs of the end users by using the open standards.

But the concept of open standards also raises difficult questions: If people are able to adapt standards to their own contexts and purposes, what, then, is standard about the standards? Exactly how much adaptation is allowed before the results differ so dramatically from the original set as to be invalid? Or is any adaptation acceptable? And who or what organization might answer these questions?

It seems clear that both universal standards and open standards have advantages and disadvantages. It seems equally clear that these concepts are based in very different values and to a great extent are thus mutually exclusive. So how would we know which concept holds the most promise for the future of the profession? To answer this question, we may turn to Robert Stake (1981), who wrote:

> To be respected, group standards should not depart far from local norms. The 55 mph speed limit, based on good reasoning, has not been a good group standard because it is too removed from common sense. What is common sense differs from place to place. I think it makes sense for standards to vary from place to place, too. Uniformity [cf. harmonization discussed in Chapter One] is an administrative virtue easily offset by the practicality of honoring local norms [p. 150].

Stake appears to be saying that the further away the standards for evaluation get from where people live and work, the less likely they will be useful and the more likely they could be harmful to the people who are intended to be the ultimate beneficiaries of our programs.

Conclusion

This issue has described standards development in a variety of international settings. The boundaries of evaluation are continually expanding, and more so as international agencies operate across borders and cultures. It is by engaging in broad-based discussion of these standards in progress that all evaluators may better understand their own standards and expand their thinking to a broader, more expansive view of their practice. In coming years, the international evaluation community may have some important decisions to make regarding the direction of standards. It is important for all evaluators to understand the complexities of the issues and how they can potentially play out to benefit all of the stakeholders whom we serve.

References

Joint Committee on Standards for Educational Evaluation. *The Program Evaluation Standards.* (2nd ed.) Thousand Oaks, Calif.: Sage, 1994.

Russon, C. "The Tao of Evaluation." *Japanese Journal of Evaluation Studies,* 2003, 3(2), 159–168.

Stake, R. "Setting Standards for Educational Evaluators." *Evaluation News,* 1981, 2, 149–152.

Taut, S. "Cross-Cultural Transferability of the Program Evaluation Standards." In C. Russon (ed.), *The Program Evaluation Standards in International Settings.* Kalamazoo: Evaluation Center, Western Michigan University, 2000.

CRAIG RUSSON is an evaluation manager with the W. K. Kellogg Foundation in Battle Creek, Michigan.

INDEX

Patton, M. Q., 17, 22, 25, 57
Pawson, J. M., 45
Personnel Evaluation Standards (JCSEE), 19
Piontek, M. E., 22
Poverty, 80
Practicality, 77*t*
Preskill, H., 24
Principles, 5
Professional development, 11–12
Program evaluation. *See* Evaluation
The Program Evaluation Standards in International Settings (Taut), 5
Program Evaluation Standards (JCSEE), 5, 8–9, 18–26, 76–77
Project Standards Measurement Instrument (PSMI), 86
Propriety guidelines, 63–64
Psychologists, 45

Quality, of evaluation. *See* Evaluation quality
Questions, 27

Raj, G., 6
Rawls, J., 27
Realistic evaluation, 45
Regional monitoring, 61
Rehabilitation, 81
Reliability, 18
Renger, R., 24
ReNSE. *See* Niger Monitoring and Evaluation Network (ReNSE)
Reporting, 72–73
Rist, R. C., 32
Rose, K., 71
Rossi, P. H., 15, 16, 17, 19, 24, 25, 46
Rothmayr, C., 32
Rouge, J.-C., 3, 11, 55, 91
Rugh, J., 3, 79, 91
Russon, C., 2, 3, 5, 6, 8, 9, 21, 26, 56, 57, 58, 89, 91
Russon, G., 3
Ryan, B., 68, 75

Sahara Desert, 55
Sanders, J. R., 15, 16, 17, 19, 20, 22, 25
Schwab, O., 34
Schwartz, S. H., 5
Scoping risks, 72
Scott-Little, C., 24
Scriven, M., 17, 22
Self-evaluation, 47, 70
SenGupta, S., 21, 24

Serdült, U., 32
Service orientation, 50–51
SEVAL Standards, 32–33, 36–40
SFE Charter, 34, 36–40
Shadish, W., 6
Sharp, C. A., 68
Shuhla, L., 2, 15, 27, 91
Small business support, 81
Small, D., 40
Smith, N. L., 26
Smith, P. B., 5
Social program benefits, 10–11
Social programs, 17
Society, protection of, 10
Socioeconomic development programs, 50
Sociologists, 45
Southern African Development Bank, 58
Speer, S., 2, 43, 44, 45, 47, 51, 91
Spinatsch, M., 32
Stake, R. E., 10, 11, 24, 25, 92
Stakeholders, 38, 72, 84
Standardized testing, 16–17
Standards: benefits of, 1, 10–11; costs of, 10–11; definition of, 5; development approaches for, 1–2; development of, 17–19, 89–90; ethical statements as, 12–13; implementation of, 90–91; as indicators of developmental stages, 43; origin of, 15–19; overlap of, 45; universal versus open, 7–8, 92–93; values' link to, 5
Standards for Evaluators of Educational Programs, Projects, and Materials (JCSEE), 18
Stern, E., 35, 48
Stockmann, R., 33
Student Evaluation Standards (JCSEE), 19
Stufflebeam, D. L., 1, 6, 15, 17, 18, 24, 25, 27, 38, 49
Summa, H., 35
Summative metaevaluation, 13
Swiss Evaluation Society, 32–33
Switzerland, 32–33, 36–40

Tasmania, 68
Taut, S., 5, 33, 92
Technology, 16–17
Textbooks, 19, 45
Thévoz, L., 32
Thompson, B., 18, 22, 24
Thompson-Robinson, M., 21, 24
Tilley, N., 45

Topical interest groups (TIGs), 20
Torres, R. T., 22, 24
Toulemonde, J., 31, 35
Transnationalism, 6
Transparency, 77t
Trotman, I. G., 68, 73
Tyler, R. W., 15

U.K. Evaluation Society (UKES), 35, 36–40
U.N. Capital Development Fund, 8
U.N. Development Programme, 57
U.N. Evaluation Group, 60
UNICEF, 56, 58, 59–60
United Kingdom, 35, 36–40, 44–45
United States: changing conditions in, 19–21; characteristics of, 16; origin of standards in, 15–19
Universal standards, 7–8, 92–93
University of the West Indies, 8
Utility guidelines, 62–63, 77t
Uusikylä, P., 52

Values, 5, 11
Vedung, E., 45
Victorian Department of Primary Industry, 74

Virtanen, P., 52
Vocational training and education (VET), 43–45
Vogel, S. M., 22
Voluntary standards, 90–91

W. K. Kellogg Foundation, 8
War on Poverty, 17
Weiss, C. H., 17, 22
Western Europe. See Europe
Western Michigan University, 12
Whitmore, E., 24
Widmer, T., 2, 26, 31, 32, 33, 40, 50, 52, 91
Williams, K., 35, 48
Wilson, R. J., 27
Winston, J., 68
Wittmann, W. W., 31
Women, 81
World Bank, 12, 56, 57
World Trade Organization (WTO), 7
World War II, 17, 18
Worthen, B. R., 15, 16, 17, 19, 25

Yarbrough, D., 2, 15, 22, 91

Zambezi River, 55

Back Issue/Subscription Order Form

Copy or detach and send to:

Jossey-Bass, A Wiley Company, 989 Market Street, San Francisco CA 94103-1741

Call or fax toll-free: Phone 888-378-2537 6:30AM – 3PM PST; Fax 888-481-2665

Back Issues: Please send me the following issues at $29 each

(Important: please include series initials and issue number, such as EV101.)

_____

_____

_____

$ _____ Total for single issues

$ _____ SHIPPING CHARGES: SURFACE   Domestic   Canadian

First Item	$5.00	$6.00
Each Add'l Item	$3.00	$1.50

For next-day and second-day delivery rates, call the number listed above.

Subscriptions: Please __start __renew my subscription to *New Directions Evaluation* for the year 2 _____ at the following rate:

U.S.	__Individual $80	__Institutional $175
Canada	__Individual $80	__Institutional $215
All Others	__Individual $104	__Institutional $249

For more information about online subscriptions visit
www.interscience.wiley.com

$ _____ Total single issues and subscriptions (Add appropriate sales tax for your state for single issue orders. No sales tax for U.S. subscriptions. Canadian residents, add GST for subscriptions and single issues.)

__Payment enclosed (U.S. check or money order only)

__VISA __MC __AmEx #_____ Exp. Date _____

Signature _____ Day Phone _____

__ Bill Me (U.S. institutional orders only. Purchase order required.)

Purchase order # _____

Federal Tax ID13559302   GST 89102 8052

Name _____

Address _____

Phone_____ E-mail _____

For more information about Jossey-Bass, visit our Web site at www.josseybass.com

NEW DIRECTIONS FOR EVALUATION
IS NOW AVAILABLE ONLINE AT WILEY INTERSCIENCE

What is Wiley InterScience?

Wiley InterScience is the dynamic online content service from John Wiley & Sons delivering the full text of over 300 leading scientific, technical, medical, and professional journals, plus major reference works, the acclaimed Current Protocols laboratory manuals, and even the full text of select Wiley print books online.

What are some special features of Wiley InterScience?

Wiley Interscience Alerts is a service that delivers table of contents via e-mail for any journal available on Wiley InterScience as soon as a new issue is published online.
Early View is Wiley's exclusive service presenting individual articles online as soon as they are ready, even before the release of the compiled print issue. These articles are complete, peer-reviewed, and citable.
CrossRef is the innovative multi-publisher reference linking system enabling readers to move seamlessly from a reference in a journal article to the cited publication, typically located on a different server and published by a different publisher.

How can I access Wiley InterScience?

Visit http://www.interscience.wiley.com.

Guest Users can browse Wiley InterScience for unrestricted access to journal Tables of Contents and Article Abstracts, or use the powerful search engine.
Registered Users are provided with a *Personal Home Page* to store and manage customized alerts, searches, and links to favorite journals and articles. Additionally, Registered Users can view free Online Sample Issues and preview selected material from major reference works.
Licensed Customers are entitled to access full-text journal articles in PDF, with select journals also offering full-text HTML.

How do I become an Authorized User?

Authorized Users are individuals authorized by a paying Customer to have access to the journals in Wiley InterScience. For example, a University that subscribes to Wiley journals is considered to be the Customer. Faculty, staff and students authorized by the University to have access to those journals in Wiley InterScience are Authorized Users. Users should contact their Library for information on which Wiley journals they have access to in Wiley InterScience.